Horatius Bonar

The Song of the New Creation, and Other Pieces

Horatius Bonar

The Song of the New Creation, and Other Pieces

ISBN/EAN: 9783337006785

Printed in Europe, USA, Canada, Australia, Japan

Cover: Foto ©Thomas Meinert / pixelio.de

More available books at **www.hansebooks.com**

THE SONG

OF

THE NEW CREATION.

MURRAY AND GIBB, EDINBURGH,
PRINTERS TO HER MAJESTY'S STATIONERY OFFICE.

THE SONG

OF THE

NEW CREATION

AND OTHER PIECES.

BY

HORATIUS BONAR, D.D.

LONDON:
JAMES NISBET AND CO., BERNERS STREET.
1872.

CONTENTS.

	PAGE
The Song of the New Creation,	1
The Mountain of Myrrh,	22
Evening by Evening,	25
Homeward,	28
The Coming Reign,	30
My Mother Earth,	32
The Year's Last Moment,	37
Divine Discipline,	40
Return unto thy Rest,	42
The Purging of the Temple,	44
Truth's Ancestry,	46
The Desert Rock,	48
The Glory to be Revealed,	51
The Eternal Work,	52
The Hymn of the Dark World,	56
Laudate,	58
The Mighty God,	59
Divine Acquaintanceship,	61
The Cup of Cold Water,	62
The Last Enemy,	64
Laudate Deum,	66

CONTENTS.

	PAGE
The Hidden Cross,	67
The True Cross,	69
Doubt not,	70
Ye know not what ye ask,	72
New and Old,	74
The Heavenly Anchor,	76
Let us Draw Near,	78
The Things that God hath Cleansed,	82
What we shall be,	84
The Stone rolled Away,	85
For Ever Perfect,	90
Show us Jesus,	93
The Second Death,	95
These are the True Sayings of God,	97
The Light is Come,	99
Praise,	101
The Fountainhead of Beauty,	102
Remember Me,	104
Intercession,	105
Taken away from the Evil to come,	107
Relics of Love,	109
The Fulness of the Unseen,	111
Light of Life,	113
Wind-Songs,	114
The Days of Thy Youth,	117
Speak, for Thy Servant heareth,	122
The Just for the Unjust,	125
Furnace Heat,	127
Bread Enough and to Spare,	129
The Supper of Thanksgiving,	131
The Supper and the Advent,	134
The Master's Voice,	137

CONTENTS.

	PAGE
Human Weariness and Divine Rest,	140
The Seamless Raiment,	144
Creation's Song,	147
One Faith and Hope,	148
The Eye Opening on the Cross,	150
Early Saved,	155
To the Holy Spirit,	157
Other Gods,	159
The Winter is Past,	164
Faith and Hope,	169
I am with Thee,	170
The Drops of the Night,	172
Who is he that Condemneth?	174
Toward the Mark,	176
The Eternal Rock,	178
Lord, increase our Faith,	180
Christmas Cheer,	181
It won't be Long,	183
Come to Thy Temple,	184
Pentecost,	187
The Cross-Wearer,	189
Thou shalt know hereafter,	192
The Coming Creed,	194
The Yoke of the True Master,	196
Be Strong,	199
Beyond the Mists,	201
Elijah's Ascension,	203
The Still Small Voice,	207
For Me,	209
Know ye not?	211
Linger not,	214
The Strength of Evil,	216

CONTENTS.

	PAGE
Transformed Darkness,	219
Up the Hill,	220
Watching for the Master,	221
In Him was Life,	225
The Double Star,	227
The Light of the Risen One,	228
Enter into thy Closet,	229
Unbeginning and Unending,	230
Sabbaths,	231
Heavenly Sunshine,	233
New-Year's Hymn,	234
Surgite,	236
Psalm XXXVII.,	247
„ XXXVIII.,	253
„ XXXIX.,	256
„ XL.,	259
„ XLI.,	263
„ XLII.,	265
„ XLIII.,	268
„ XLIV.,	269
„ XLVI.,	273
„ XLVII.,	275
„ XLVIII.,	276
„ XLIX.,	279

THE SONG OF THE NEW CREATION.

> Appropinquat enim dies
> In quâ justis erit quies ;
>   Quâ cessabunt persequentes
>   Et regnabunt patientes.
>
> Dies ille, dies vitæ,
> Dies lucis inauditæ ;
>   Quâ nox omnis destructur,
>   Et mors ipsa morietur.
> OLD HYMN.

IT draweth near!
  That day,—of days the day,—
For which the Bridegroom waits,
  For which the virgins pray ;
For which earth sighs, and hastes
  To greet it on its way ;
Asking, as on it comes,
  Why this so long delay?
It draweth near at last!
  Who shall its advent stay?

It hastes to rise!
  That sun,—of suns the sun,—
Whose rising is the pledge
  Of evil all undone,
Of darkness at an end,
  And heavenly day begun;
The war of ages o'er,
  And the last battle won.
It hasteth to arise,
  Its glorious race to run.

It breathes o'er earth!
  That balm-exhaling air,
In heaven's own odours steeped,
  To a sick world to bear
The health of that pure realm,
  Where sickness is not, where
True life has its abode,
  And in which all things rare
Flourish, but never fade,
  Divinely soft and fair.

It swelleth forth!
  That song,—of songs the song,—
Creation's melody,
  From harps till now unstrung,

The new, sweet, matin hymn,
  As yet on earth unsung,
Poured in rich burst of praise
  From every heart and tongue;
The anthem of a world
  Redeemed from woe and wrong.

Behold, He comes!
  And with Him comes the love
Which makes these wastes below
  Like heaven of heavens above;
When round His central throne
  Shall all creation move;
No atom out of place,
  No will to swerve or rove;
Swayed by the silent breath
  Of the eternal Dove.

He comes in power!
  The King,—of kings the King,—
All righteousness and peace
  In His right hand to bring;
Into the last abyss
  Each rebel crown to fling;
Time's ages of misrule
  To end; that now may spring

Order and law and light
   Beneath His holy wing.

He comes in pomp!
   The holy pomp of heaven,
When sin is at its height,
   And earth is all unshriven.
Scorched by no human fire,
   No cloud-begotten levin,
His banded foes fall back,
   Before His fury driven.
The nations of the world
   Into His hand are given.

He comes in light!
   Girt with His golden zone,
Arrayed in heavenly white,
   With light his pathway strewn.
Like a long-absent Prince
   Returning to his throne;
No more disowned, unloved,
   No more unpraised, unknown,
He comes to share His light
   And glory with His own.

He speaks at last
   The word,—of words the word,—
'Lo, I make all things new!'
   And now with sweet accord
The heavens and earth obey;
   The universe is stirred
When, from the throne of thrones,
   The potent voice is heard,
'Old things now pass away,
   And Eden is restored.'

The foe is bound
   With the unbreaking chain;
The spoiler now is spoiled,
   No more o'er earth to reign;
Purged is creation now
   From the primeval stain
Of the old serpent's trail.
   Never to rise again,
The prince of evil falls,
   Slain with the mighty slain.

Death's reign is done!
   The grave gives up its dead;
The blessed sleepers wake,
   One with their blessed Head.

Life triumphs over death,
   The enemy has fled;
The tyrant of the tomb
   Is now a captive led,
Upon his head at last
   His slaughters visited.

The curse is gone!
   The blessing comes instead;
And now, where'er we go,
   On hallowed ground we tread.
The canopy of love
   Is stretched above our head;
The soil, no longer curst,
   Is like a garden spread;
The wilderness re-blooms
   With verdure overlaid.

All strife is o'er!
   Ended the world's rude jar;
And universal peace
   Succeeds the age of war.
Man's pride, and rage, and hate,
   Have gone and left no scar;
Of all that laid earth waste,
   Nothing remains to mar

The mellow calm that rests
 On all things near and far.

No sorrow comes!
 All tears are wiped away;
No shade of weariness
 On eye or brow can stay.
Each new morn's sweet song is
 The song of yesterday.
Faith's future wears no frown,
 And hope knows no delay;
No cloud of unbelief
 Absorbs one heavenly ray.

New heavens and earth,
 In holy beauty bright,
Arise and shine, like morn
 When ends the clouded night.
New heavens, and earth, and sea,
 Free from all stain and blight,
Spread out their sparkling robes,
 Their raiment clean and white;—
O region of the pure,
 Land of unknown delight!

Zion awakes,
 Jerusalem puts on

Her beauty and her strength;
  True city of the Sun,
Thy light, thy light is come;
  Ascend thy shining throne!
Thy warfare now is o'er,
  Thy enemies o'erthrown;
Wave, wave thy palm on high,
  Thy victory is won.

City of peace!
  In bridal beauty clad,
Thy day of mourning done,
  No more thy voice is sad.
Thy King is in thee now;
  He who in anger bade
Thy foes exult o'er thee,
  He who in vengeance had
Sent fire into thy towers,
  Has come to make thee glad.

O pleasant land!
  Land of the mighty too.
No cloud remains to dim
  Thy sky of stainless blue.
No lion shall be there,
  Nor beast of prey pass through;

Thy fields, and vales, and streams,
   How excellent to view!
Upon thy thousand hills
   Glistens the holy dew.

The storm is spent!
   Faint-breathing into balm;
The Master's 'Peace, be still!'
   Has wrought the blessed calm.
And now the breeze of heaven
   Sighs soft through each fair palm;
The voice of righteous men
   Swells out in each glad psalm,
Praise to the Son of God,
   Praise to the great I AM.

The sword is sheathed!
   The spear is flung aside;
The gathered hosts disband,
   And scatter far and wide.
Man's blood no longer stains
   The river's crystal tide;
The sky no longer rings
   With shouts of human pride.
'Tis universal peace,
   Each note of war has died.

Jehovah reigns!
  And now the nations praise;
The Christ of God is King;
  In righteousness He sways,
Over a happy world,
  The sceptre of His grace;
The kingdoms all are His,
  His strength the earth upstays;
His glory fills the heavens,
  His word the world obeys.

Jerusalem,
  City of sun and gold,
The dwelling of the saints,
  Descendeth, as foretold,
In words of living fire,
  By Hebrew seers of old;
Of the one flock of God,
  The everlasting fold;
Earth's tribes walk in its light
  And glory manifold.

The city shines
  In splendour from afar,
In the round firmament
  Like a new burnished star.

Eternal love within;
  No din, nor strife, nor jar:
For all of every clime
  Its pearly gates unbar;
Peace walks its golden streets,
  Fled every sound of war!

No sun by day!
  By night no moon they need;
Jehovah is their light,
  From mist and darkness freed.
The Lamb upon the throne
  Is all the light they need;
He to the wells of life
  Daily His own doth lead;
And on His pastures green
  Sweetly His own doth feed.

Clear flows the stream
  From the supernal throne;
Stream of eternity,
  All heavenly streams in one;
Whose waters carry life
  And freshness all its own,
With immortality
  And gladness now unknown.

Upon its banks are heard
  The songs of joy alone.

Blessed are they
  Who to the great repast,
The supper of the Lamb,
  Are called, that they may taste
The heavenly viands there;
  Who at that table rest,
Drinking in all its love,
  Reclining on the breast
Of Him who is Himself
  The Master and the feast.

No night is there!
  No shadow ever falls
Upon thy golden streets,
  Or stains thy jasper walls.
No watchman on thy towers
  The night-hours nightly calls;
No plunderer of the dark
  The startled ear appals.
'Tis endless festival
  Within thy princely halls.

Thy citizens
  No coming sunset dread;
Above them the mild light
  Of a soft sky is spread,
No more by wasting storms
  To be revisited.
Nor age nor siege they fear;
  All enemies have fled.
The glory now returns
  To rest above thy head.

The tree of life
  Yieldeth its endless store;
Twelve harvests year by year.
  The palm and sycamore,
The olive of the hills,
  Old Judah's tree of yore,
No beauty had like this,
  Nor such abundance bore;
Its very leaves are life
  And health for evermore.

The Cross has won!
  The Galilean now
Has conquered in the fight.
  For us He smote the foe,

For us He led the war,
  And laid the strong one low.
His blood hath washed the earth,
  And purged all things below;
Earth's glory now is His;
  Its crown is on His brow.

The song goes up!
  From every breathing thing
Upon the holy soil
  From which th' old serpent's sting
Has been for ever plucked;
  Streams, hills, and forests bring,
In sweetly swelling strains,
  Their happy offering;
And praises everywhere
  Ascend to earth's one King.

Glory to God!
  Glory to Christ the Lord;
Glory in earth and heaven,
  Glory with one accord;
To Him who earth upholds
  By His almighty word;
To Him by whom all things
  Have been at last restored!

His is the name of names,
  In heaven and earth adored.

Thrice-happy earth!
  Guilty, but now forgiven;
From which has been expelled
  The all-defiling leaven.
Oh what a day is thine,
  The brightest of the seven!
The day of days, ere long
  To be in mercy given,
When heaven shall be on earth,
  And earth shall all be heaven.

Thrice-happy earth!
  All perfect and all fair;
Which of the orbs above
  May once with thee compare?
Gem of the universe!
  The seat of beauty rare;
Dear home of love and truth,
  Of all things perfect, where
Reigneth the righteous King,
  Creation's Lord and Heir.

Thrice-happy earth!
   Henceforth the first and best
Of handiworks divine;
   Once ruined and unblest;
Now washed and beautified,
   The place of God's own rest
Throughout the eternal age,
   In splendour manifest,
As the one blood-bought orb,
   The island of the blest.

Great mystery!
   Among the orbs that are
Sparkling above in light;
   Of all, or near or far,
The brightest and the best:
   Once seat of woe and jar,
The least and loneliest;
   Now with no sin to mar,
It rolls in new-born glow,
   The one redeemèd star.

Thy fellows shine,
   Each in his own clear light;
But not like thine their glow,
   So exquisitely bright;

On which has never shone
  A love so infinite
As that which thou hast found,—
  The love which washes white
Sin's stain, and into day
  Turns the profoundest night.

Upon *their* soil
  No cross has ever stood.
They have no Bethlehem,
  And no incarnate God.
They have no Golgotha,
  And no all-purging blood;
No lamb of sacrifice,
  No cleansing laver-flood;
No priestly word of peace
  Making all evil good.

'Tis not *their* soil
  (Though with all beauty stored,
And sparkling with fair light,
  As all with one accord
They speak their Maker's praise),
  Of which the eternal Word
Took part, and upon which
  His blood divine was poured.

B

They cannot claim to be
   Of kindred with their Lord.

They cannot say,
   'Twas here He lived and died,
And here upon this tree
   For us was crucified.
This earth of ours alone,
   Of all the orbs beside,
The million orbs of space,
   Can claim to be allied
To Godhead; and to heaven
   So firmly, sweetly tied.

Their history,
   Great though perchance it be,
And full of miracle,—
   The wondrous history
Of more stupendous orbs
   Sweeping in majesty
Round wider, stranger depths
   Of vast infinity,—
Is not like ours, so fraught
   With heavenly mystery.

This earthly orb
  Is dull, and poor, and small;
Thick clouds engirdle it
  Like a funereal pall.
It wheels through narrow space
  An obscure silent ball;
And to a thousand suns
  Is debtor still for all
The daily, nightly lights
  That gently on it fall.

Yet to this globe
  All Godhead has come down;
Here is the link divine
  That knits the upper throne
To creaturehood below,
  Never to be undone!
This world, long wandering
  Without a star or sun,
That seemed for ever lost,
  Is now for ever won.

For ever won!
  Plucked from the power of sin,
And made all holiness.
  Now with the sons of men

God's tents for ever pitched!
　No shadow of a stain;
On all Creation's round!
　The old destroyer slain;
And now at last begun
　The pure and holy reign.

The reign of right
　Supplants the sway of wrong;
The reign of promised peace
　To earth has come: the long
Long era of the blest!
　With now unloosèd tongue
The nations utter praise;
　Earth's broken harp is strung,
Creation now is glad,
　And sings its ancient song.

Earth is all new!
　A beauty now is given
Greater than what it lost;
　Its fetters all are riven;
Creation is set free,
　And the dark spoiler driven
From his usurpèd seat;
　The foul, corrupting leaven

Of evil is purged out,
    And earth is one with heaven.

Most holy place!
    O beauty ever fair;
O fields that never fade,
    O rich and balmy air;
O home for ever freed
    From weariness and care;
O halls in which the robes
    Of festival they wear!
No dread of coming change
    Disturbs the gladness there.

New heavens, new earth!
    Knit sweetly into one,
No more to separate.
    The ancient curse is gone;
With no sad seed of death
    Thy purgèd soil is sown;
Thy seas no tempests know,
    Thy skies no clouded sun;
God's purpose is fulfilled,
    The age of evil done!

THE MOUNTAIN OF MYRRH.

UP to the fair myrrh-mountain,
    The fresh frankincense hill,
I'll get me in this midnight,
    And drink of love my fill.
O hills of fragrance, smiling
    With every flower of love;
O slopes of sweetness, breathing
    Your odours from above!
Ye send me silent welcome,
    I waft you mine again;
Give me the wings of morning,
    Burst this still-binding chain:
        For soon shall break the day,
        And shadows flee away.

Amid time's angry uproar,
    Unmoved, unruffled still,
Keep, keep me calmly, truly,
    Doing the loved One's will.
'Mid din of stormy voices,
    The clamour and the war,
Keep me with eye full-gazing
    On the eternal star;

Still working, suffering, loving,
  Still true and self-denied,
In the old faith abiding,
  To the old names allied :
    For soon shall break the day,
    And shadows flee away.

From earthly power and weakness
  Keep me alike apart ;
From self-will and unmeekness,
  From pride of lip or heart.
Without let tempests gather ;—
  Let all be calm within,
Unfretted and unshaken
  By human strife and sin.
And when these limbs are weary,
  And throbs this sleepless brain,
With breath from yon myrrh-mountain
  Revive my soul again :
    For soon shall break the day,
    And shadows flee away

There my beloved dwelleth,
  He calls me up to him ;
He bids me quit these valleys,
  These moorlands brown and dim.

There my long-parted wait me,
   The missed and mourned below;
Now, eager to rejoin them,
   I fain would rise and go.
Not long below we linger,
   Not long we here shall sigh;
The hour of dew and dawning
   Is hastening from on high:
      For soon shall break the day,
      And shadows flee away.

O streaks of happy day-spring,
   Salute us from above!
O never-setting sunlight,
   Earth longeth for thy love;
O hymns of unknown gladness,
   That hail us from these skies,
Swell till you gently silence
   Earth's meaner melodies!
O hope all hope surpassing,
   For evermore to be,
O Christ, the Church's Bridegroom,
   In Paradise with thee:
      For soon shall break the day,
      And shadows flee away.

EVENING BY EVENING.

Advesperascit ; et inclinavit dies.

GOOD night, ye gems of beauty,
   Good night, thou gentle blue;
On quiet bed I lay me,
   And bid farewell to you.
Good night, ye wakeful woodlands,
   Good night, ye sleeping flowers,
Amid whose smiles and odours
   I've passed day's wayward hours.
Good night, ye star-tipt mountains,
   Old friends, the tried and true;
Good night, ye wandering waters;
   Ocean, good night to you.
      Good night to all, but not to Thee,
      My God, who ever art with me.

Good night, dear faces round me,
   Night's hours will swiftly run;
And we shall say, Good morning,
   At the ascending sun.

The farewell hour is coming,
　　The last good night is near,
When I shall part in silence
　　With those who love me here.
Then, all my farewells over,
　　Just passing out of sight,
Unweeping and untrembling,
　　I'll *look* my last good night.
　　　　Good night to all, but not to Thee,
　　　　My God, who ever art with me.

Yet not good night for ever;
　　For He who is my day
Will wake me soon;—I see Him
　　Already on His way.
No, not good night for ever;
　　I shall but sleep in Him,
Who shall arouse me early,
　　While yet the dawn is dim,—
Who shall arouse me early,
　　And bid this flesh arise,
In glorious resurrection,
　　To meet Him in the skies.
　　　　Good night to all, but not to Thee,
　　　　My God, who ever art with me.

I see Him,—lo, He cometh!
    Himself the morning light,
To bring the dawn of gladness,
    The dawn that knows no night.
O Bridegroom of the morning!
    Bright bringer of the day,
Put on Thy fair adorning,
    Thy beautiful array.
Lord Jesus, star of evening,
    Yet star of morning too;
Earth's uncreated splendour,
    Rise on our longing view.
        Good night to all, but not to Thee,
        My God, who ever art with me.

HOMEWARD.

TO my beloved ones my steps are moving;
    Not hard the road that ends in love and
        home.
Have done my eyes, have done my feet with
    roving;
  'Tis to the well-known gate I look and come.

Your watch is now on the eternal mountains;
  Our eyes are gazing upward from afar.
Your rest is now by the clear-welling fountains;
  Ours is the journey still, the toil and war.

Years have gone by since the last words were
    spoken;
  O loved and saved, how gladly shall we meet
In the home-city, where no ties are broken,
  Where love is perfect, fellowship complete!

I see your crowns, the wreaths which cannot
    wither,
  And from the city-walls ye beckon me;

'Come up, and tarry not. Oh, come up hither,
    To this dear land of light we welcome thee!'

Only a little while: a little longer
    Of tarriance here upon these death-swept
        plains.
O well-beloved, death is growing stronger,
    And life more feeble in these ebbing veins.

To follow you we are each day preparing;
    And where you are, there we shall shortly be.
Death is to us but as an angel, bearing
    The keys of life and immortality.

Yet not the less we say, 'Twere surely better
    That He should come and summon us away
To meet Him in the sky, ere yet the fetter
    Of dark corruption bind our crumbling clay.

Then ye who slept, and we who knew no
    sleeping,
    Should meet together each to tell his tale;
The tale of earthly weariness and weeping,
    The short strange story of Time's cloudy vale.

Come then, Lord Jesus, come! Thy church is
    calling;
The world is old, though still its skies are
    blue.
Its flowers are fading, and its leaves are falling;
    Come in Thy glory to make all things new.

THE COMING REIGN.

KING of kings! ascend Thy throne;
    Visit this Thine earth again;
Gird Thy sword upon Thy thigh;
    Take Thy mighty power, and reign.

King of nations! claim this world
    With its kingdoms for Thine own.
Raze each rebel fortress here,
    Level every hostile throne.

King of Israel! now arise,
    And rebuild Thy Salem's walls;
Gather Jacob's scattered flock;
    Hear Thine Israel when he calls.

King of saints! Thy ransomed own,
   They the members, Thou the head;
Speed the great deliverance,
   First-begotten of the dead.

King of glory! King of heaven!
   King of earth! arise and reign;
All creation sighs for Thee;
   Visit Thine own earth again.

King eternal! Son of God!
   Earth and heaven shall Thee obey;
Principalities and powers
   Own Thine everlasting sway.

MY MOTHER EARTH.

MY mother earth,
    From which we sprang,
And into which ere long
We shall return,
For a far higher birth,
When weakness shall put on
Immortal strength, and from the urn
Our ashes shall arise,
Meet for unfading skies;—
We look into thy depths,
And see in them,
Not death, but life;
As if an angel sat
In shining garments there,
As in the tomb of old,—
The wondrous sepulchre
Of Him who died our death,
And rose in raiment fair,
Our everlasting life.

O mother earth!
    Out of whose dust I came,

And into which I am
So swiftly to return;—
On thy green turf I sit,
And, touched by it,
I seem to gather vigour to my frame.
Of life, not death, thou art the nurse;
Of all fruit-bearing things
Thou art the bounteous source.
To thee the seed goes down,
And dies in darkness; from thee springs
Again more beautiful, bright wings
From thee receiving, to arise in joy.
To thee we too go down,
And rest in silence for a little hour,
Till, like the tree or flower,
We rise anew in resurrection-power.

My mother earth!
Not even amid the snows
And ice that wrap thee round,
When frost has chilled the ground,
And winter holds thee fast
In bitter chains, and when the blast
Sweeps o'er thy shivering plains,
Shall I be kept from thy embrace,
Or shrink from thy pale marble face.

Winter has slain thee, and all life
Seems to have left thy veins.
But shall I shun the breast
Of my dead mother laid to rest?
Shall I forbear to kiss
The well-known countenance,
Or leave thee in the grasp
Of the destroying foe?

My mother earth!
  Thy spring shall come again;
  Thy April shall return,
  And all thy May behind it, when the rain,
  Mingled with happy sunshine, shall come down,
  And quicken earth.
  For thee the blessed hope of rising shines,
  When summer shall bring gladness to the soil.
  For us the hope too shines;
  My mother earth!
  Thou canst not be my tomb.
  Thou canst not hold me in thy icy chains.
  I shall arise,
  When thou shalt have dissolved my dust,

And in dissolving ripened it;
Making it purer and more fit
For the eternal paradise.

My mother earth!
All beautiful around,
Fragrant in every vale;
With melody of sound
Rejoicing everywhere;
The blue above,
The green beneath;
The mighty arch,
Filled with its marvellous clouds,
Cheered by its joyous winds,
Or awed by its dread storms.
The ever-murmuring wood,
The ever-whispering grove,
The solitary glen or moor,
The wayward, wilful stream
Gushing with eager haste
Through its dark moss-green glen;
The purple of the moorland waste,
The yellow stretch of level sand,
The multitude of shining waves,
Swept shoreward to the sloping strand.

My mother earth!
  How fair, and full, and great!
  All beauty covers thee,
  All riches fill thy depths;
  O'er thee the mighty sun
  Leans in the loving warmth
  Of his unfailing beams;
  O'er thee the mother-orb of night
  Flings her unspotted veil;
  And round thee gathers close
  The matchless robe of flowers
  That covers and adorns thy loveliness,—
  The beauty of the ever-varying year.

My mother earth!
  He whose creating hand
  Both made and moulded thee;
  He who pronounced thee good,
  And gave thee that bright sun,
  And these fair hills and vales,
  Made thee for endless years;
  Not for the melting fire,
  Or the submerging flood,
  Or for the abode of ill,
  Or for a place of graves,
  Or for a land of pain;

But for eternal joy,
For endless righteousness,
For holy blessedness,
For the great seat and home
Of everlasting light,—
Of endless love!

———o———

THE YEAR'S LAST MOMENT.

THE crowd sweeps onward still:
    And we with it move on,
Part of the ever-rushing multitude;
    Till the great goal be won,
And for the last time sinks the ever-setting sun.

Another hour has struck,
    With solemn note, and slow;
Another fragment of time's cliff has rushed
    Into the vale below;
Another of earth's streams this moment ceased
    to flow.

Another lamp of time
    Has flickered into gloom,
And left us lonelier in our lonely watch,
    Waiting the light to come ;
Not *into*, but *beyond*, the life-devouring tomb.

Another of time's stars
    Has vanished from the eye ;
Ah ! now the light of the immortal dawn
    Is coming up the sky,
And quenching, one by one, these midnight
    gems on high.

Another headland turned,
    While bends the quivering mast ;
Another beacon of the lone, lone sea
    Our vessel has shot past.
The shore, the shore is near ! Is that the
    haven at last ?

Another bridge of life
    Has now been crossed : few more
Remain for us ; another ridge of time
    We've reached, from it to explore
The far-outspreading green of the not distant
    shore.

Another pillar fallen
  In Time's old temple! See
How fragment upon fragment darkly lies;
  And hear how heavily
The echoes wind along by the slow-swelling
    sea!

Another song has closed,
  A true but varied strain,
And the deep-turret chime I hear afar
  Has echoed out Amen,
Swelling the long-drawn fall of the well-known
    refrain.

Oh, well for us to watch!
  Our night will soon be o'er;
The day of mortal doom approaches fast,
  The Judge is at the door;
Awake! arise, my soul, and sleep thy sleep
    no more!

DIVINE DISCIPLINE.

Patior ut videam.

I SUFFER, that I may behold, when pain
   Has passed away, Thy face in righteous-
ness.
It is the suffering here that fits the soul
   For the bright vision of eternal bliss.

I suffer, that these dim, dim eyes of mine
   May be thus purified, and made to see
Afar off even now, and farther still,
   In the vast vistas of eternity.

Only the touch of suffering can remove
   This earth-born dulness from my narrow
     sight;
Only the healing which the rod imparts
   Can fit me for beholding holy light.

I suffer, that I may behold the cross
   In all its fitness for a soul like mine;
Who but a sufferer knows what such a cross
   Can mean, or see its glory fully shine?

DIVINE DISCIPLINE.

I suffer here, that I may taste the joy
    Hereafter in the city of the blest;
That I may bear the brilliance that shall burst
    Upon us in the Paradise of rest.

Our present light affliction, which endures
    But for a moment, worketh for us there
A weight of glory, such as sorrow here
    Alone can fit us to possess or bear.

Only the pressure of a loving hand,
    A hand as tender as divinely wise,
Can lift these drooping eyelids, and impart
    True health and vigour to these sickly eyes.

I suffer, that I may be strong to gaze
    Upon the glory yet to be revealed;
Glory which we shall yet in joy behold,
    When earthly vision shall be purged and healed.

O silent arrows of the Lord my God,
    O secret touches of a hand unseen,
O sharpness of the sweet but bitter rod,
    Yet softness of the still small voice within!

RETURN UNTO THY REST.

In uno quies.

AMONG the many, I am lost and weary;
    They do not take from me the deep
        unrest.
They make me but more lonely and more
        dreary;
    They promise fair, but cannot make me blest.

This heart, thus trying in a thousand centres,
    To find an orbit round which it may roll,
Comes back depressed, taught by these vain
        adventures:
    One centre only stays the restless soul.

Only in One is rest for us; true quiet
    For the vexed human heart is from above:
Though far removed from toil, and brawl, and
        riot,
    It cannot rest itself in creature-love.

Earth is all motion and disquiet; only
    In One above, who changes not nor moves,
We find repose: there tranquil, but not lonely,
    We rest in One who ever, ever loves.

Life is all tempest, o'er time's ocean ranging;
    A troubled morning, and an angry even:
Only in One is anchorage unchanging,
    Only in One is the eternal haven.

Creation rocks; all that is made is moving;
    The strongest, brightest, goodliest, and best:
In *One*, the ever-fixed and ever-loving,
    In *One* I anchor, and in *One* I rest!

THE PURGING OF THE TEMPLE.

John ii. 16.

TAKE these things hence!
    Self and its idols vile,
    The sin and vanity,
    The lust of gold and gain.

Take these things hence!
    Each folly of the will,
    Each unsubdued desire,
    Each fever-pulse of earth.

Take these things hence!
    The love of earthly ease,
    The unchecked appetite,
    The impulses of time.

Take these things hence!
    The self-will and the sloth,
    Vainglory of the mind,
    Ambition of the soul.

Take these things hence!
    The love of creature-love,
    The images of sense,
    The passions of the world.

Take these things hence!
    The pride of place and pomp,
    Of dress and ornament,
    Of luxury and gems.

Take these things hence!
    Lusts of the ear and eye,
    Lusts of the mind and flesh,
    That fill up all the room.

Take these things hence!
    The passions and the dreams!
    The idle hopes and fears,
    The impure mirth and song.

Take these things hence!
    Let not the holy shrine,
    The temple of the Lord,
    Be thus defiled and stained.

Take these things hence!
    Make not my Father's house
    A house of merchandise,
    The market of the world.

Take these things hence!
    The Holy Spirit's shrine,
    God's holy house, are ye;
    And ye are not your own!

TRUTH'S ANCESTRY.

Ego sum hæres apostolorum.—TERTULLIAN, *de Præscr. hæret.* ch. xxxvi.

THE old is better than the new,
    The oldest still the best;
And on that oldest of the old
    My stedfast faith I rest.

I rest where righteous men of old
    Their resting-place once made;
The promise of the woman's seed
    To crush the serpent's head.

That is the oldest of the old,
   Yet newest of the new;
In every age the light of time,
   In every age the true.

Its date is the eternal age,
   When its first sparkle shone;
It is the oldest of earth's stars,
   And yet its youngest sun.

For ever fresh, and good, and fair,
   It shineth as it shone:
The 'always,' 'all,' and 'everywhere,'[1]
   Is found in it alone.

Of God's great love to guilty man
   It brings the blessed seal:
The serpent's bruisèd head fore-speaks,—
   Messiah's bruisèd heel.

Love from the everlasting love
   It brings, earth's wounds to cure.
Of war against man's foe it tells,
   Of victory made sure.

---

[1] 'Semper, ubique, et ab omnibus.'—VINCENTIUS of Lirins, *Against Heresy*, ch. ii.

'Herein is love,' it writes upon
   The gates of Paradise.
'Herein is love,' it writes upon
   Each burning sacrifice.

Oldest and truest creed! In thee
   We find the love of God
Upwelling at the altar's base,
   And reaching us through blood.

THE DESERT ROCK.

They drank of that spiritual rock that followed them; and that rock was Christ.—1 COR. x. 4.

ROCK of the desert, pouring still
   Thy stream the thirsty soul to fill;
Rock of the desert, now as full
   Of living water, pure and cool,—
     We stand beside thee now.

Rock of eternity, to thee
In thirst and weariness we flee;

Thy waters cannot cease to pour,
Their fulness is for evermore.
  Let him that thirsteth come!

Bright water of eternity,
We come, we come to drink of thee;
  The voice of welcome that we hear,
  The voice dispelling every fear,
    Is 'whosoever will.'

River of life, upon thy brink
We sit, and of thy waters drink.
  The murmur of thy sparkling wave
  Speaks still of Him who came to save,
    Who bids us drink and live.

River of peace, so full and bright,
Each drop clear-shining with the light;
  And still the voice that comes from thee,
  The voice that telleth all is free,
    Is 'whosoever will.'

River of health, thy current pours
Its freshness on these leprous shores:

True Jordan, bidding all draw nigh
For health and immortality,
  With 'whosoever will.'

River of love, so deep and wide,
All heaven is in thy flowing tide:
  For all the love of God is here,
  The love that casteth out all fear,
    The 'whosoever will.'

Dear river, what a sun is thine!
What glories on thy waters shine,
  What freshness in each sparkling drop!
  And still the voice that cometh up
    Is 'whosoever will.'

River of God, still flowing on!
Thy source the everlasting throne.
  River of heaven, translucent stream,
  Thy fulness ever at the brim
    For 'whosoever will.'

THE GLORY TO BE REVEALED.

Exoriar aliis.

SINKS the swift sun; yet sinks but to arise
    In other regions far beyond our sight:
We follow him with dim and dazzled eyes,
    Till every ray is quenched in silent night.

We miss him, but he comes not; he has gone
    To show his glory in more cloudless air:
Nothing is lost to him, for in that zone
    He puts on raiment more serenely fair.

So sinks the child of heaven, when to our eye
    He disappears; he does not die, but live.
He has passed out beyond this narrower sky,
    Diviner splendour to receive and give.

He sinks to rise; he sets to shine again
    In fairer heavens, and with diviner light;
No more to set, or take on cloudy stain,
    Or leave behind another world of night.

O cloudless heaven, in which we hope to shine,
  When we shall leave behind us this dim
    sphere!
O glorious world, all holy and divine,
  Where we shall sparkle through the eternal
    year!

———o———

THE ETERNAL WORK.

Vitæ melioris in usum.

I LAY up treasure in the heavens;
  My gold accumulates and grows.
I hoard, but not on earth; my wealth
  Before me daily goes.

My hands, my lips, each power within,
  I fain would educate for heaven.
Here is the school where we are trained,
  And here the lessons given.

I shall not die at death, nor shall
  My past of life all useless be;

These powers within me, lodged by God,
　　Are for eternity.

This is the seed-time, here the seed;
　　I pass into the soil and spring;
But far above me, out of sight,
　　Is the bright blossoming.

'Tis for eternity I read,
　　And do, and think, and study here;
Pruning and purging every branch,
　　That it may fruitage bear.

Not leaves without the fruit, nor yet
　　Fruit without leaves; but side by side,
The leaf and fruit; and both through Him
　　In whom I here abide.

What God hath given me, that I count
　　Too precious and too great to lose;
And all I have I treasure up
　　For everlasting use.

My little garden-plot of life,
　　Though poor, must all be duly tilled;

Its future is a vast unknown,
　　And I must see it filled.

I work that I may fitted be
　　For more than angel's work above;
When of this life's strange mystery
　　The meaning I shall prove.

By earthly discipline and toil
　　I sharpen these my blunted powers,
For nobler work awaiting them
　　In vaster fields than ours.

For I have other fields above
　　To reap, when autumns here are done;
And so my sickle would I whet
　　For harvests yet unknown.

And all this discipline of time,
　　The pain, the weariness, the strife,
Tells on my endless usefulness
　　In the unmeasured life.

What here I learn will one day tell;
　　What I shall reap I now must sow;

And nothing shall be lost of all
  This varied life below.

A higher and more useful life
  Above, shall mine for ever be;
And all that I have learned on earth
  Shall then be used for Thee.

In higher service shall I then
  These renovated powers employ;
Work without weariness be mine,
  And everlasting joy.

THE HYMN OF THE DARK WORLD.

L IGHT of the world! All the earth is waiting,
    Looking and sighing for the promised day.
Dark are the heavens; still the east is clouded,
    Hidden in gloom the glory of Thy ray.

Age upon age has been slowly rolling,
    Since by the seers thy splendour was foretold;
Thickens the gloom on the pagan mountains,
    Deepens the silence over Judah's fold.

Sorrow and evil all the nations cover;
    Errors and idols hold their blinding sway;
Truth its head hideth, and the Book of blessing
    Seems like a treasure vilely cast away.

Heralds of gladness vainly lift their voices;
    Human ears are closed; human hearts are sealed.

THE HYMN OF THE DARK WORLD.

Who hath received love's last sweetest message?
  Where has Jehovah's great arm been revealed?

Dark is the night over Asia's millions;
  China and India still sit in the gloom:
Sad is the shade over islands and islands;
  Earth's fairest gardens are cold as the tomb!

Egypt, Arabia, Elam, sit in shadow;
  Africa knows not the tidings of light;
Europe lies gloomy; half cloud and half sunshine;
  Deep o'er the vales of Greece rests the long night.

Hope of the longing! All creation groaneth,
  Loathing her bondage, longing to be free;
Stretching her hands out for the promised freedom,
  When the thick shadows all shall rise and flee.

Joy of the world! Days and nights of darkness,
  Silent and sorrowful, here have rested long:

Hasten Thy one never-ending day-spring,
  End all these ages of time's grief and wrong.

Speed the glad tidings! 'Tis finished, 'tis finished!
  He who hath died for us liveth again.
Send over earth the love and the brightness;
  Take to Thee, Lord, Thy great kingdom, and reign.

---o---

LAUDATE.

COME, all ye nations, utter all your praises!
  Come, all ye churches, sing aloud to God!
Come, all ye saints of every tribe and kindred!
  Come, all creation, sound His praise abroad!

Give to Jehovah everlasting praises,
  Glory and honour to the Father give;
Glory and honour to the Son and Spirit,
  Glory to God, in whom we move and live.

With the glad singing heaven aloud is ringing;
   Not a voice is silent, and shall earth be dumb?
Praise Him, land and ocean; praise Him,
   rock and river;
Come with one lip and heart; joyfully come.

Give to the slain Lamb everlasting glory,
   Now to the risen Christ hearts and voices
   raise;
Give to the crownèd King honour and blessing,
   Power and dominion, and glory and praise.

THE MIGHTY GOD.

ASCRIBE ye strength to God!
   The mighty Lord is He,
   The God of majesty,
   Jehovah is His name;
   O'er all the earth His fame;
   Ascribe ye strength to God!

His strength is in the clouds!
   Girded with glorious might,
   Compassed about with night;

Yet light His dwelling-place,
And light in all His ways.
His strength is in the clouds!

He rideth on the heavens!
  The heaven of heavens is His,
  With all its light and bliss;
  His are the stars of light,
  His is the solemn night.
He rideth on the heavens!

Sing loud to God our strength!
  Rejoice and praise His name,
  Rejoice and sound His fame;
  Rejoice and tell His grace,
  Rejoice before His face.
Sing loud to God our strength!

His kingdom knows no end!
  The King of kings is He,
  The Lord of lords is He,
  The God of gods is He,
  The Judge of earth is He.
His kingdom knows no end!

DIVINE ACQUAINTANCESHIP.

ACQUAINT thyself with God!
   Know thou His tender love;
So shall the healing sunshine fall
   Upon thee from above.
Acquaint thyself with God!
   In Him alone is peace,—
Rest for the weary child of time,
   And everlasting bliss.

Acquaint thyself with God!
   Choose thou the better part;
So shall His heavenly sunlight be
   The day-spring of thy heart.
Acquaint thyself with God!
   He bids thee seek His face,
That thus thy youthful soul may taste
   The sweetness of His grace.

Acquaint thyself with God!
   In Jesus and His cross
Read there that love which makes all loss
   But gain, all gain but loss.

Acquaint thyself with God
  In childhood's joyous prime;
So shall thy life a foretaste prove
  Of heaven's long summer-time.

———o———

THE CUP OF COLD WATER.

MATT. X. 42.

POOR stranger, in the Master's name
  This cup of water thus I give;
Lift it to thy parched lips, and may
  Its freshness all thy thirst relieve.

I know thee not, lone stranger, save
  As one of the dear Christian band;
Take then this cup I offer thee,
  As from His own beloved hand.

For He, in whose loved name I give
  This cup, has pledged His royal word,
That even for a deed like this
  There shall be yet a bright reward.

THE CUP OF COLD WATER.

A member of Thy body, Lord,
   Thus in Thy name I would relieve;
And what I give to him, as Thine,
   To Thee, O Master, thus I give.

It is *Thy* thirst that I relieve,
   Even Thine, O everlasting Lord;
For what we do to these Thine own,
   We do to Thee, unseen, unheard.

This water, quenching one saint's thirst,
   How bright it sparkles in Thine eyes!
Each drop, thus given, Thou writest down,
   Awarding it a heavenly prize.

THE LAST ENEMY.

Nunc impar et uni.

WE yield to death ; the fight is lost,
   When the last enemy assails.
Against ten thousand we had fought ;
   Now *one*, and he *unseen*, prevails.

The sting of death is sin ; 'tis this
   That makes us feeble in the fight :
We shrink and flee ; but all in vain ;
   We cannot face that foe of might.

And yet in yielding do we win ;
   Vanquished in this last mortal strife,
We conquer him who conquered us :
   Through death we enter into life.

The grave becomes to us the gate
   Of glory through eternal years ;
And through the clouds that veil the tomb,
   Our resurrection-sun appears.

The sun of an eternal morn,—
  Morn of the mistless and the bright!
The sun of an eternal noon,
  That knows no sunset and no night.

Then shall defeat be all reversed,
  And I the conqueror at last:
My heel upon the head of death,
  My mortal strife for ever past.

My Captain is the Prince of Life!
  He leads me on, He leads me in;
Wounded and baffled oft I am,
  But the great field at length I win.

Who fights with death must take the wounds
  He took when fighting here below:
Who conquers death must share the tomb
  Of Him who overcame our foe.

LAUDATE DEUM.

Te invocamus,
Te adoramus,
Te et laudamus,
 O beata Trinitas!

ETERNAL Father, gracious One,
 With whom all fulness is alone:
Only a blessing such as Thine
Can fill an empty soul like mine.

Eternal Son, eternal love,
Shed down Thy healing from above:
 Hear us, when on Thy name we call,
 O Thou who art the 'all in all.'

Eternal Spirit, life and light,
Health, gladness, comfort infinite,
 On us Thy needy ones below,
 From Thy celestial stores bestow.

Eternal God, to whom we bow,
Father and Son and Spirit Thou;
　　To Thee eternal praise be given
　　From men and angels, earth and heaven.

———o———

THE HIDDEN CROSS.

THREE hours the land was wrapt in gloom,
　　Three hours the city saw no sun;
Three hours blank fear was in each face;
　　It seemed as if earth's day were done.

Three hours the cross itself was hid;
　　While through the gloom the Sufferer's cry,
'My God, why dost Thou me forsake?'
　　Breathed out His dying agony.

Three hours in that mysterious cloud,
　　That blotted out the noonday sun,
The face of God's dear Son was hid;
　　Only the ear could hear His groan.

Most wondrous hours, in which was done
    The greatest deed e'er done below:
The deed in which all heaven was joined,
    That saves us from the endless woe.

Unveil that cross to me, O Lord,
    That I may see the sacrifice
There offered, and in it the way
    To a recovered Paradise.

Light up that cross to me, O Lord,
    That I its heavenly power may know;
The health, the pardon, and the joy
    Which from its open fountain flow.

Earth has no sun to light it up!
    These eyes are dim, the scales remove;
Straight from itself the light must come,
    That shows me all its grace and love.

Unveil that face to me, O Lord,
    Once hid in darkness for my sin;
That in its light I may rejoice,
    And with true boldness enter in.

Withdraw each cloud that hides the cross;
   Let nothing come between that face
And this faint heavy eye of mine,
   That longs to see its heavenly grace.

---o---

THE TRUE CROSS.

WE glory only in the cross,
   On which the Son of God
Finished the mighty sacrifice,
   Purging our sins with blood.

There peace for ever made by God,—
   Himself our peace, we see;
Himself the bearer of our guilt
   On the great altar-tree.

The reconciling work was done,
   The work that ends the strife,
When He, the Word made flesh, for us
   Laid down His human life.

The debt was paid, the peace was made,
   The veil was rent in twain,
And access to the Father given,
   By Him the victim slain.

We come then boldly to the throne:
   With a true heart we come,
Emboldened only by the blood
   Which speaks the 'Welcome home!'

———o———

DOUBT NOT.

O YE of little faith,
   Why stand ye thus without,
Distrusting all my grace,
   Oppressed with fear and doubt?

Do justice to my love,
   Put each hard thought away;
Wrong not my faithful word,
   No longer lingering stay.

Why hold ye back in fear,
  As if I were untrue?
Are not my words sincere?
  And are they not for you?

Remember ye my tears
  Wept o'er Jerusalem?
The tears of Man and God,—
  Was not my love in them?

Behold this mercy-seat
  On which I sit: draw near;
Take from my pierced hand
  All that thou needest here.

Trust me for every want
  Of body and of soul;
And hear the blessed words,
  'Thy faith hath made thee whole.'

YE KNOW NOT WHAT YE ASK.

YE know not what ye ask!
    The cup of which I drink,
Can ye too drink of it,
    Or taste its bitterness?

Ye know not what ye ask!
    This baptism of mine,
Can ye partake of it,
    Or bear my agony?

Ye know not what ye ask!
    My vinegar and gall;
The nails, the crown of thorns,—
    These, these are not for you.

Ye know not what ye ask!
    The stripes and buffetings,
The reed and robe of scorn,
    The shouts of mockery.

Ye know not what ye ask!
    Know ye Gethsemane?

YE KNOW NOT WHAT YE ASK.

    Or know ye Golgotha,
        The darkness and the tomb?

Ye know not what ye ask!
    My cross ye cannot bear,
    My load ye cannot take;
        They are for me, not you.

Ye know not what ye ask!
    The cup of which I drink,
    I drink alone for you:
        Its bitterness is mine.

Ye know not what ye ask!
    My baptism of woe
    I undergo for you:
        Its awfulness is mine.

Ye know not what ye ask!
    The crown shall yet be yours;
    But mine must be the fight,
        And mine the victory.

NEW AND OLD.

THAT which hath been is now;
    The *now* repeats the *long ago*.
'Twas the old sun of Paradise,
Unchanged, we saw this morning rise,
    In all its ancient glow.

And that which is to be,
    On earth it hath already been;
The future will repeat the past,
And as the first shall be the last,—
    Ages of change between.

The loathsome fatal sin
    Of man, it hath been long ago;
Sin's penalty of death and pain
Have held earth in its iron chain
    For ages dark of woe.

The wondrous love of God
    To man, it hath been long ago;

It is, and it shall be revealed,
Though long in mystery concealed:
  Earth with that love shall glow.

The Paradise of God
  Hath been, and yet again shall be,
In beauty on this tarnished earth,
When at Creation's second birth
  Death and the curse shall flee.

Once the first Adam reigned,
  Ere earth had known the deadly stain;
Soon the last Adam shall appear,
And with His church in glory here,
  Begin the holy reign.

THE HEAVENLY ANCHOR.

HEB. VI. 19.

SURE anchor of the soul!
  The hope that knows no shame;
Which rests upon the mercy-seat,
  Immoveably the same.

Hope resting upon love!
  What tempest can us part?
Thou canst not change with changing years,
  Nor cheat the trusting heart.

Sure anchor of the soul!
  My faith lays hold of thee;
Thou canst not drag, nor part, though fierce
  The storm upon my sea.

Hope, fixed within the veil
  Where love has its abode;
Love, sealed with blood, and flowing from
  The bosom of our God.

Hope given to us by love,—
    A love which finds its way
Through the great channel of the cross,
    And turns our night to day.

No power of wave or wind
    Can loose the stedfast grasp
Of our tossed vessel in the storm,
    Or faith's sure chain unclasp.

That which can sweep through heaven,
    And the great throne assail,
Alone can touch thee where thou art,
    Firm fixed within the veil.

In evil days of storm
    This anchor holds us still;
Firm fastened to the mercy-seat,
    We dread no power of ill.

We cannot drift nor sink,
    In life and death secure;
We ride upon the breaker's crest,
    And yet feel calm and sure.

Bright hope, fair mercy-seat!
　　We keep our hold of you;
Through each day's tossing of the deep,
　　We have you still in view.

———o———

LET US DRAW NEAR.

NO distance now! the far-off and the near
　　Have met in peace around the one dear
　　　cross;
The Jew and Greek, the free and bond are here,
　　Counting all loss as gain, all gain but loss.

The hour is come! men worship now the
　　Lord
　　No longer at Jerusalem alone;
But over all the earth, with one accord;
　　True worshippers of Him whose name is One.

Into the holiest by the blood we go,
　　Boldly along the new and living way;

Our conscience purged, our vesture fair as snow,
　Our earthly night exchanged for heavenly
　　day.

With the true heart and the sure faith we come,
　Sprinkled, and purged, and made all over
　　clean ;
No evil conscience whispering doubt or gloom,
　Without no shadow, and no dread within.

In through the veil we pass without a fear;
　The rich-wrought veil, that guarded once
　　the door,
Now rent in twain, invites us to draw near,
　And tread with reverent joy the holy floor.

The golden mercy-seat stands full in sight,
　Our High Priest seated there dispensing
　　grace,
The ark, the cherubim, the glory bright,
　With incense filling all that holy place.

One Christ, one cross, one sacrifice, one Priest,
　One altar, and one temple for us all ;

One Spirit in whose common love we rest,
   One God and Father on whose name we call.

One love descending from one common Lord,
   One love ascending from ten thousand souls;
One brightness from on high upon us poured,
   One song of praise for ever upward rolls.

Son of the Blessed, Christ our Lord and King,
   To Thy one everlasting mercy-seat
Thy church on earth her prayers and wants
     would bring,
   Round it the ransomed multitudes now meet.

Creation's root and centre, around whom
   God's universe of being, far and wide,
Shall yet be seen revolving, when the gloom
   Shall pass away of time's dull eventide.

Thy church's Head and Bridegroom, in whose
     love
   Thy chosen bride shall yet more fully rest,
When the fair heritage below, above,
   Shall be revealed, in spotless glory drest.

Thy Israel's God and Lord, the builder up
  Of Thy Jerusalem's long-broken wall,
When from her lips shall pass the bitter cup
  She gave Thee once, the wormwood and the gall.

Faith finds Thee near, and walks with Thee below,
  Without the shadow of a cloud or gloom;
Hope sees the crown upon Thy piercèd brow,
  All earth renewed, and the great kingdom come.

THE THINGS THAT GOD HATH CLEANSED.

Acts x. 15.

"Ὕπνον δέχεται, ἵνα καὶ ὕπνον εὐλογήσῃ· τάχα καὶ κοπιᾷ, ἵνα καὶ τὸν κόπον ἁγιάσῃ· τάχα καὶ δακρύει, ἵνα τὸ δάκρυον ἐπαινετὸν ἀπεργάσηται.—GREG. NAZ. *Orat.* 31.

BY sleep He consecrated sleep,
   And taught us how to lay our head,
With trust like His, divine and deep,
   In slumber on our nightly bed.

By death He consecrated death,
   And made the grave a holy home,
In which our flesh, the turf beneath,
   Shall rest in hope until He come.

Resting, He consecrated rest,
   And bade us in His rest to dwell,
As when, with weariness oppressed,
   He sat at noon on Sychar's well.

Weeping, He consecrated tears,
   And showed the mourner how to weep;
And yet the tear-sick eye He clears,
   Lest sorrow be too long and deep.

Born as a man is born, and laid
   In weakness on a woman's knee,
He consecrates the cradle-bed,
   Ennobling human infancy.

Loving, He consecrated love,
   Lifting it out of human sin,
Making it pure like that above,
   And deepening the fount within.

WHAT WE SHALL BE.

Paulatim plena.

ERE long we shall be full; as night by night
   Yon crescent moon fills up its silver bow,
So we fill up that fulness of pure light,
   Into whose beauty we shall hourly grow.

Slowly it fills, and yet it tarries not;
   Still adding to its curve of spotless white,
As on it rolls, suffering no cloud or blot
   To mar the growing fulness of its light.

Slowly we fill, and yet the fulness flows,
   Nor cloud nor storm its pureness can absorb;
Gently we grow, and yet the brightness grows
   Into the circle of the perfect orb.

With stedfast face yon moon still keeps its eye
   Fixed on the central sun by day, by night;
Nothing between in that translucent sky,
   And in his light grows hourly yet more bright.

Thus, with our eye on yon eternal sun,
   We fill up the full measure of our light,
Growing like Him who shineth, taking on
   Each hour the image of His glory bright.

THE STONE ROLLED AWAY.

All night upon the city wall
   The moon had hung her veil,
And o'er the slopes of Olivet
   Had flung her splendour pale.

On Golgotha's dark blood-steeped turf
   All night her beams had shone:
'Twas silence then; the groans had ceased;
   The shouting crowd was gone.

All night within the rocky tomb
   The holy body lay,
Until the messenger from heaven
   Announced the rising day.

From heaven, ere morn awoke, he came,
  On mightier errand sent
Than to light up another star
  In that clear firmament.

To roll away the stone he came,
  Which sealed the wondrous tomb,
In which the immortal One had lain
  Shut up in mortal gloom.

Man's hands had hewn the virgin rock,
  Man's hands had placed the stone ;
But that which rolls it back must be
  An angel's hand alone.

Down from the highest heaven of heavens
  He comes to break the seal ;
Without a word, to thrust aside
  The Roman sentinel.

He rolls it back, and takes his seat
  In silence on it there ;
His countenance the lightning flash,
  His robe divinely fair.

THE STONE ROLLED AWAY.

Upon that stone of earth he sits
    In silence, there to wait
Till the three days' imprisoned King
    Shall issue from the gate;—

That rocky gate, misnamed of death,
    From which comes forth in power
The First-begotten of the dead,
    Death's mighty Conqueror.

So cometh still to us from heaven
    A blessed angel oft,
A gentle messenger of light,
    With footstep fair and soft.

Oh, many and many a stone from us
    Has thus been rolled away:
It seemed too vast for us to touch,
    As o'er the gate it lay.

When we awoke at early dawn,
    We said with troubled heart:
Who shall roll back the ponderous stone,
    Or bid our fears depart?

As we went forth, we found with joy
    The dreaded care had flown;
We saw no hand, we heard no voice,
    And yet the stone was gone!

And on it sat an angel fair,
    All heaven upon his face;
He pointed to a risen Lord,
    And spoke sweet words of grace.

And all the day our hearts were light,
    With holy gladness gay;
The dreaded thing had taken wing;
    The stone was rolled away.

That which shut in our gracious Lord,
    And hid Him from our sight,
Was gone; and Jesus had come forth,
    The Prince of Love and Light.

The stone for ever rolled away,
    The angel sitting there,
Were pledges of a heavenly grace
    That banished all our care.

THE STONE ROLLED AWAY.

Oh, on how many an earthly grief
   Or fear, a light unknown
Has, with a joyful suddenness,
   In heavenly glory shone!

To many a tomb of earthly tears
   Comes one of heavenly mien;
On many a gloomy stone of life
   An angel sits unseen.

Yes, thus, when the sweet morning's sun
   Night's ravelled brow unknits,
On many a stone of earth below
   A gentle angel sits.

Fresh from the heavens he has come down,
   And on the massive stone
Which he has rolled away he rests,
   To watch the rising sun.

And with the rising sun he goes
   His work to do for man;
The daily work of heavenly love
   Which only angels can.

FOR EVER PERFECT.

QUICKLY bright life withers,
    Quickly fond ones part;
Quickly links are broken,
    Binding heart to heart.

Slowly grief departeth,
    Slowly wounds are healed;
Slowly joy returneth,
    Slowly blanks are filled.

Is there no high region
    Where life never dies,
Where the love remaineth
    In beloved eyes;—

Where no stars are falling,
    Where no thunders chide,
Where no sun is scorching,
    And no streams are dried;—

Where no winter freezes,
    And no spoiler strips

July's summer roses
　From beloved lips ;—

Where no foreheads wrinkle,
　And no locks are grey ;
Where we see no dear ones
　Dying day by day ;—

Where the deathbed moaning
　Is a thing unknown,
Where no hands are graving
　Names upon the stone ;—

Where the May is endless,
　And the noons all clear ;
Where the beauty shineth
　Round the summer year ;—

Where the love-linked circle
　Never snaps in twain,
And the household mirror
　Taketh on no stain ;—

Where no picture, hanging
　On ancestral halls,

Bright with mellow sweetness,
   Long lost love recalls;—

Where no garden flower-plots
   Weed-bewildered stand,
And the untrained roses
   Show the broken band?

Yes, there comes a region
   Where our life shall be
Health in all its freshness,
   Immortality!

Where the breathing fragrance,
   On the holy hills,
Tender and untainted,
   Heavenly strength distils;—

Where the grave is rifled
   Of its precious store,
And each mound is levelled,
   To be raised no more.

SHOW US JESUS.

LEAD us, O Lord, to Bethlehem;
    Show us the child there born,
  The Son to us there given:
There show us Christ the Lord,
Reveal the love of God.

  Take us, O Lord, to Nazareth;
    Show us the tender plant,
  The root from the dry ground:
There show us Christ the Lord,
Reveal the love of God.

  Lord, guide us to Gethsemane;
    Show us the sweat of blood,
  Make known the agony:
There show us Christ the Lord,
Reveal the love of God.

  Lord, bring us on to Calvary;
    Display the cross of shame,
    Show us the sacrifice:

There show us Christ the Lord,
Reveal the love of God.

Lord, take us to the empty tomb,
   And say, He is not here;
   Lo, He is risen indeed:
There show us Christ the Lord,
Reveal the love of God.

Place us at last on Olivet,
   Whereon His feet shall stand
   When He shall come again:
There show us Christ the Lord,
Reveal the love of God.

THE SECOND DEATH.

Prima mors animam nolentem tollit à corpore; secunda animam nolentem tenet in corpore; ab utrâque morte id habetur, ut quod non vult anima de suo corpore patiatur.—AUGUSTINE.

THEY die, and die not; theirs is life in death,
  And death in life; a living death for aye:
Done with earth's sunshine, done with heaven's fresh breath,
  Shut in with utter darkness, and shut out from day.

They might have lived; for He who loved and died
  Came with the words of immortality.
But Him they would not hear, when by their side;
  And now His grace has passed beyond their reach away.

Now death, the death that dies not, has become
    Their dismal heritage in realms below.
O endless deathbed! O eternal tomb!
    O never-coming bliss, but ever-coming woe!

O second death! the death of life, and all
    That makes life worth the living! O thou deep,
Deep sadness of the soul's dread funeral,
    At which, if angels can, they sure must ever weep.

To them the resurrection comes in vain.
    It comes; but to the death of deaths they rise,—
The second death, the death of deadly pain,
    From which all hope departs, from which all comfort flies.

O Thou, the sinner's hope, ere hope be gone,
    Save Thy lost creature from that death of doom.
Oh, pluck the prey from the destroying one;
    Oh, raise him, raise him now from sin's sad prison-tomb.

THESE ARE THE TRUE SAYINGS OF GOD.

SURE the record; Christ has come!
  Rich, for us became He poor.
O my soul, then know His love;
  Love Him, serve Him evermore.

Sure the record; Christ has died,
  Bearing on the cross our sin;
Is not this the gate of life?
  Son of Adam, enter in!

Sure the record; Christ is risen,
  He hath broken every chain:
Silent stands the empty tomb,
  Never to be filled again.

Sure the promise; Christ will come,
  Though the promise lingers still:
Heavy seems the wing of time,
  Weary with the weight of ill.

Signs are mustering everywhere,
    And the world is growing old;
Love is low and faith is dull,
    Truth and right are bought and sold!

Then when men are heedless grown,
    And the virgins slumber all,
When iniquity abounds,
    Then He cometh, Judge of all!

Cometh He to raise His own,
    Wipe the tear from every eye;
Cometh He to right the wrong,
    Trodden truth to lift on high.

To dethrone the lie of lies,
    Each dark falsehood to destroy;
To begin the age of light,
    Earth's long sighed-for Sabbath-joy.

THE LIGHT IS COME.

O UT of darkness into light
　　Jesus calls the sons of night;
Out of midnight into day
Jesus bids us come away.
　　　Arise! arise and shine!
　　　　Thy light, thy light is come;
　　　The glory of the Lord
　　　　Is risen upon our gloom.

From the prison-house of sin,
From the foes without, within;
From this mortal weariness,
Jesus calls to joy and peace.
　　　Arise! arise and shine!
　　　　Thy light, thy light is come;
　　　The glory of the Lord
　　　　Is risen upon our gloom.

From this world's alluring snares,
From its perils and its cares,

From its vanity and strife,
Jesus beckons us to life.
   Arise! arise and shine!
      Thy light, thy light is come;
   The glory of the Lord
      Is risen upon our gloom.

From the vanities of youth,
Into rest, and love, and truth,
Into joy that never palls,
Jesus in His mercy calls.
   Arise! arise and shine!
      Thy light, thy light is come;
   The glory of the Lord
      Is risen upon our gloom.

PRAISE.

PRAISE ye the Lord, all things that be!
  Sky, sun, and moon, with every star;
All things above, below, Him praise,
  In whom we live, and move, and are.
    Praise ye the Lord!
    Praise Him with one accord;
      Praise Him for evermore.

Praise ye the everlasting God!
  The God of majesty and might;
The God of grace, and truth, and love,
  The God of glory infinite.
    Praise ye the Lord!
    Praise Him with one accord;
      Praise Him for evermore.

Praise Father, Son, and Holy Ghost,
  The one Jehovah, God, and Lord;—

    Creator of the earth and heaven,
      For ever be His name adored.
        Praise ye the Lord!
        Praise Him with one accord;
          Praise Him for evermore.

---o---

THE FOUNTAINHEAD OF BEAUTY.

I WAS in love with hill and vale,
  The noon's warm flush, the star-light pale,
The murmur of the midnight gale,
  The mirth of wayward streams.
I wooed the silence of the night,
The blushes of the bursting light,
The sea's green depths, the heaven's blue height,
  And days went by in dreams.

I sought the shadows of the wood,
I woke the glen's low solitude;
I mused above the mountain-flood,—
  Days of the rock and grove!

The tide's great ebb and flow, to me
Was speech, and psalm, and minstrelsy;
O musical and mighty sea!
    Young life went by in love

And shall I cease to love you now,
Ye hills above, ye rocks below,
Because I see your beauty flow
    From God the only wise?
Shall I not love you, praise you more?
And fill me with your beauty's store,
The glory of earth's wondrous shore,
    And splendour of its skies?

When faith has now restored to me
All childhood's dear simplicity,
And, in heaven's own sweet liberty,
    Made me once more a child;
When, standing by the cross, I read
All nature in the light thence shed,
No darkness and no guilty dread,—
    Bright with the undefiled.

REMEMBER ME.

Nihil apud Deum tutius supplicante.—ENNOD. EP.

NOW at the Father's side,
    On the eternal throne!
But once in infant-weakness laid
In lowly Bethlehem's manger-bed,
    Child of a woman born!
        Jesus the Christ, the Son of God,
        Remember me.

Now in the heaven of heavens,
    Worshipped by angels high!
But once upon the earth beneath,
With sinful men in Nazareth,
    And devils in the waste!
        Jesus the Christ, the Son of God,
        Remember me.

Now 'mid eternal songs,
    Thyself the glorious theme,—

The once derided here,
Object of scoff, and taunt, and sneer,
   Bearing the curse for us!
      Jesus the Christ, the Son of God,
         Remember me.

———o———

INTERCESSION.

Quare tu, verbi minister, interim insta et munito muros et turres Hierusalem, donec et te invadant. Vocationem et dona agnoscis. Ego pro te unice oro; si quid potest (sicut non dubito) oratio mea. Tu ergo mutuum redde, et portemus invicem onus istud. Nos soli adhuc stamus in acie; te quærent post me.—
LUTHER TO MELANCTHON.

WHEN it is well with thee before thy God,
      Remember those with whom it is not well;
Bear them upon thy heart before that God
   In whose glad presence thou hast learned to dwell.

Pray for thy friends: let the full heart go out
   For all thou lovest here; forget not one:

Count o'er the precious names; nor let a doubt
   Obtrude that God upon thy cry can frown.

For the dear church of God thy prayers pro-
   long,
   The one wide family of God below,
The little flock of every tribe and tongue;
   All one in faith, in love, in joy and woe.

For all the many members of that throng,
   And for each fellow-pilgrim lone and faint;
Known or unknown, the feeble or the strong,
   For each hard-pressed and sorrow-stricken
   saint.

Plead for the bleeding heart and burdened soul,
   Plead for the weary and the wounded here;
Ask that the God of health would make them
   whole,
   And the great Comforter dispense His cheer.

Plead for the weary earth, upon whose breast
   Ages of evil and unrighteousness
Have lain, unbroken by one hour of rest;
   Plead for the hast'ning of the age of peace.

Plead for the advent of the promised King,
　　The reign of heavenly glory here on earth,
The budding of the world's eternal spring,
　　The coming of creation's second birth.

---o---

TAKEN AWAY FROM THE EVIL TO COME.

HE died to live; for Jesus died:
　　He lives, to die no more.
Why weep for one whose tears are dried,
　　For whom all death is o'er?

You miss the little footstep here,
　　You miss the golden smile;
You miss the sunny locks so fair,
　　You miss the playful wile.

Yet all is well; you part to meet
　　And clasp your gem once more,
When all shall deathless be, and sweet,
　　On the eternal shore.

In the first opening stage of life
    The little traveller failed;
Too rough the road, too full of strife,—
    The gentle spirit quailed!

He laid him down to sleep, and slept
    In smiling sleep away:
He waked not, though we called and wept;
    He would not,—would not stay.

Gently he sighed, and gently sank
    Ere morning had begun;
Closing his eyes as if he shrank
    From gazing on the sun.

In the first storm the little bark
    Went down beneath the foam;
In its first flight the little lark
    Soared to its kindred home.

RELICS OF LOVE.

THE farewell is complete; the grave
    Is waiting for the dead:
Only the tresses we retain
    That graced that gentle head.

All else is gone; corruption's touch
    Has quenched her lustre now:
These shine as fresh as when they fell
    Like sunbeams o'er her brow.

The eye, the lip, the smile are gone;
    But ye with us still stay:
Ye are the amaranths of love,
    That moulder not away.

O tresses of the beauteous dead,
    Fair locks with lilies twined;
All that remains of loveliness,
    Like sunbeams left behind.

Like daylight left on golden clouds,
    When fades the evening light;
The one dear relic of the face
    That made our home so bright.

Leave us these relics of our child,
    The braid of silken hair
That hung above the azure eye,
    So sparkling and so fair.

We cannot always bear the sight,
    And yet we would not part
With these sweet fragments of a form
    So treasured in our heart.

We gaze, and then we turn away,
    And then we gaze again;
Then turn away, and lay them by,
    Till time has soothed the pain.

One more embrace, another sound,
    Though but a passing sigh,—
That would be bliss, another glance
    Of the beloved eye.

For this we wait; hope is not dead:
    We look above this gloom
To the bright morn when we shall meet
    In light beyond the tomb.

---o---

THE FULNESS OF THE UNSEEN.

IN vain, in vain with human love
    To fill this longing heart I strove.
A stranger to the joys above;—
    It would not thus be filled!
In vain, in vain on earthly ground
I sought what could not here be found,
The healing of a hidden wound;—
    It would not thus be healed!

In vain, in vain I tried to roll
Life's load to some dim, distant goal,
To feed on dust a famished soul;—
    It would not thus be fed!

Created beauty was a dream,
Created love a fair, fond gleam,
Created joy a fitful stream ;—
    It would not always flow!

O loveliness of time, how poor!
O gay, gay world, how soon your store
Is emptied, to be filled no more!—
    Thou canst not soothe nor cure.
O Christ of God, alone in Thee
All beauty, love, and joy I see;
My all shalt Thou for ever be;—
    Thou canst not change nor die!

LIGHT OF LIFE.

LIGHT of life, so softly shining
From the blood-besprinkled tree,
Never waning nor declining,
    Shine, shine on me!

Light of life, so sweetly gleaming
Down upon our troubled sea,
With the love of Jesus beaming,
    Shine, shine on me!

Light of life, that knows no fading;
From all changes Thou art free.
Holy Light, that knows no shading,
    Shine, shine on me!

Light of life, that knows no setting,
Day and night Thy beams we see,
Joy and peace in us begetting,
    Shine, shine on me!

Light of life, in childhood's gladness,
To Thy radiance we would flee;
Be our strength in days of sadness,
   Shine, shine on me!

Light of life, all health bestowing,
Lift we up our eyes to Thee;
From the cross of Jesus flowing,
   Shine, shine on me!

———o———

WIND SONGS.

Luctantes ventos, tempestatesque sonoras.—VIRG. *Æn.* i. 54.

SING, ancient wind,
   That hauntest this old hill;
As in forgotten days,
   Draw out thy music still:
Keep time to the rich notes
   Of this old moorland rill.

Sing through the forest firs,
   Sing through the garden-flowers,

Through the broad forest-oak,
   And through the fragrant bowers,
Through the high battlements
   Of these half-fallen towers.

Sing round the ocean-cliff,
   Sing o'er the swelling wave;
Sing down the lonely vale,
   And o'er the leaf-strewn grave;
Sing past the hollow arch
   Of the far-echoing cave.

Sing o'er the harvest field,
   And down the shaded stream;
Sing through the network bright
   Of summer's twilight gleam,
When gold and silver mix
   Like colours in a dream.

Sing through the olive-boughs,
   The palm-groves of the plain;
Sing through the broken shafts
   Of temples cleft in twain;
Sing through the ruined aisles
   Of each long-silent fane.

Sing o'er Arabia's sands,
  And through Judæa's hills;
Sing amid Horeb's rocks,
  Or up the leaping rills
Which bounteous Lebanon
  Out of his fulness fills.

Sing past Moriah's mount,
  The mount of festival;
Sing through old Salem's streets,
  And echo through each hall,
The wail of ages long
  At her sad funeral.

THE DAYS OF THY YOUTH.

GIVE thou thy youth to God,
   With all its budding love;
Send up thy opening heart to Him,
   Fix it on One above.

He seeks thy heart, my child,
   He wants to make thee blest;
Thy soul with His own joy to fill,
   To give thee peace and rest.

Be early wise for heaven,
   Choose thou the narrow way;
The gate is strait, the road is rough,
   But it will end in day.

Shun the vain, giddy crowd!
   Its shows, and snares, and lies;
Above its beauty and its love,
   Lift thou thy wandering eyes.

Set thou thy heart on truth!
    The way of truth is one.
Shun error, sweet though it may be;
    Look upward to the sun.

One Sun there is above,
    One sun of light below;
Take the one light from the one Sun,
    So shall thy light o'erflow.

Love thou the book of God,
    Prize every holy line;
Steep in its truth thy thirsty soul,
    And claim each hope as thine.

Know thou the God of love;
    Seek thou thy joy in Him,
A joy that shall endure and bless,
    When other joys grow dim.

Take thou the side of God,
    In things or great or small;
So shall He ever take thy side,
    And bear thee safe through all.

Aim high! thou wert not made
   To grovel on the ground:
Aim high! this life is not the last;
   The higher lies beyond.

Quail not before the bad,
   Be brave for truth and right;
Fear God alone, and ever walk
   As in His holy sight.

Each stroke the marble moulds,
   And every touch the clay;
Each sunbeam rising from the deep
   Unfolds the gorgeous day.

So does each little word,
   Or wish, or deed, or plan,
Each hour's impression, help to give
   Form to the future man.

Shun what is low or mean,
   Be generous and true;
The noble models of the past,—
   Keep them before thy view.

Stoop not to brood on self,
   Check the self-pitying tone;
Rise above self and selfish thoughts,
   And learn to stand alone.

Alone, with only God
   For guidance and for light,
For wisdom and for sympathy,
   For counsel and for might.

Love the broad fields of earth,
   Its ever mirthful flowers;
The fragrance of its waving boughs,
   Alike in sun and showers.

Love all that God hath made,
   Each bud, each leaf, and gem;
They shine all fair in Him, and He
   Shines beauteously in them.

Read thou the real and true,
   Lest thou become a lie,
Thy life a fiction, and thy words
   Mere words of mockery.

Dread unreality,
  And be what thou dost seem:
The true is fairer than the false,
  Whatever men may dream.

Be real to thyself,
  Be real to thy God,
Be real to thy fellow-men;
  Keep thou the one true road.

Bend the expectant knee,
  Love the still hour of prayer;
Go to the seat of God, and pour
  Thy heart's deep fulness there.

Seest thou yon cross afar?
  There died the Son of God:
That cross, it leads and beckons thee
  Along the heavenly road.

SPEAK, FOR THY SERVANT HEARETH.

SPEAK Thou to me, O Son of God,
    And let my spirit hear Thy voice;
Speak with Thy still small voice of love,
    And let this heart of mine rejoice.

Speak, as Thou didst when here on earth,
    The words of everlasting love;
That my whole soul may yield to Thee,
    And in Thy steps with gladness move.

Take full possession of this heart,
    Leave there no part untouched, unfilled;
Withdraw each veil that hides Thy face,
    And let Thy glory be revealed.

Tell of Thy love and grace, O Christ,
    Tell of Thy ever-cleansing blood;
Tell of Thy cross and sacrifice,
    And draw this longing heart to God.

Put forth Thy power, O mighty Lord,
   Break down this proud rebellious will:
Root out the unbelief within ;
   O teach me, teach me to be still.

Say, 'I am thine,' and teach me, Lord,
   To answer with a glad Amen ;
Teach me to say, 'And I am Thine,
   Thou fairest of the sons of men.'

Say, 'Peace I leave with thee, my peace
   To thee for evermore I give :'
Say, 'I am life, my life is thine,
   I live, and ye shall also live.'

Abide with us and in us, Lord,
   Help us to keep Thy cross in view;
Oh tell us all Thou art, and say,
   'Abide in me, and I in you.'

Put Thy left hand beneath my head,
   Let Thy right hand embrace me still ;
Oh bring me to Thy festal hall,
   And let me drink of love my fill.

Oh speak the word, 'Rise up, my love;
    Rise up, my fair one, come away:
The rain is o'er, the winter past,
    The flowers appear, 'tis May, 'tis May!'

Speak to the day, and it shall break;
    Speak to the shadows,—they shall flee:
Then shall we see Thee as Thou art,
    And be for ever, Lord, with Thee.

THE JUST FOR THE UNJUST.

> In te mortem mors necavit ;
> Dum se ipsum immolavit
>   Vera Christus hostia.—OLD HYMN.

THE Son of God descends ;
    The promised Child is born ;
The eternal Word becometh flesh ;
    Shineth the star of morn !

He lives a human life ;
    A human death He dies ;
Lies buried in a human grave,
    The accepted sacrifice.

He riseth from the tomb,
    And leaveth in His stead
The mortal wrappings of the flesh,
    The raiment of the dead.

He took our place below,
    We take His place on high :

He lived that we might live, He died
    That we might never die.

Through Him we come to Thee,
    O God of holy love!
He is the way, the truth, the life,
    Oh fix our hearts above!

Our life is in Thy love;
    Without it all is night:
Life is not life without Thy love;
    Thy friendship is our light.

FURNACE HEAT.

Good is Thy will, O Lord, and good Thy way;
   Good is Thy discipline, though now so sore.
Good is Thy guidance in this evil day;
   Good will all soon appear, when on the shore,
   Landed and safe, we shall be tried no more.

Not joyous now, but grievous, are Thy strokes;
   And yet their fruit is purity divine.
Thy rod we need; yet more Thy power and skill
   To mould, according to Thy fair design,
   Thy perfect likeness in us line by line.

Yet spare us, spare us, for the flesh is weak,
   And the poor spirit shrinks beneath the rod;
Now it is willing, then it fails and faints
   Beneath the pressure of the heavy load,
   Asking: And must we suffer thus, O God?

And yet we dare not ask a lighter load,
   A gentler discipline, a smoother way,
An easier life on earth, a sweeter cup,
   A tenderer touch in moulding this hard clay!
Teach us to trust, to suffer, and obey.

We place ourselves within Thy holy hands,
   Saying, Not our will, Lord, but Thine be done!
All that we need Thou knowest, O our God:
   Give what we need, yet spare each feeble one
   What may be spared, and yet the kingdom won.

BREAD ENOUGH AND TO SPARE.

The bread wherewith I have fed you in the wilderness.
—Ex. xvi. 32.

FOOD of the soul, eternal bread,
    Which whoso eateth never dies;
Upon these desert sands spread out,
    The hidden manna of the skies.

True bread of heaven, and bread of God,
    In thee we find eternal store:
To thee in our deep need we come;
    Give us thyself for evermore.

True bread of life, the Father's gift,
    To feed the famished sons of earth;
Who eateth of thee hungers not,
    Even in this land of human dearth.

Life of the dead, O living Christ!
    Pour in Thy life into our death,

That we, all faint of soul, may know
    The power of Thine all-quickening breath.

Quickened by Thee, no death we fear;
    Sustained by Thee, our weakness turns
To strength immortal; touched by Thee,
    Our coldness into fervour burns.

Fed at Thy table, we are filled;
    Each day repeats the sweet repast,—
Sweeter and sweeter still, for Thou
    Keepest the best unto the last.

THE SUPPER OF THANKSGIVING.

FOR the bread and for the wine,
    For the pledge that seals Him mine,
For the words of love divine,
    We give Thee thanks, O Lord.

For the body and the blood,
For the more than angels' food,
For the boundless grace of God,
    We give Thee thanks, O Lord.

For the chalice whence we sip
Moisture for the parchèd lip,
For the board of fellowship,
    We give Thee thanks, O Lord.

For the feast of love and peace,
Bidding all our sorrows cease,
Earnest of the kingdom's bliss,
    We give Thee thanks, O Lord.

For the heavenly presence-bread,
On the golden table laid,
Blessed banquet for us made,
    We give Thee thanks, O Lord.

For the paschal lamb here given,
For the loaf without the leaven,
For the manna dropt from heaven,
    We give Thee thanks, O Lord.

Only bread and only wine,
Yet to faith the solemn sign
Of the heavenly and divine!
    We give Thee thanks, O Lord.

For the words that turn our eye
To the cross of Calvary,
Bidding us in faith draw nigh,
    We give Thee thanks, O Lord.

For the words that fragrance breathe,
These poor symbols underneath,
Words that His own peace bequeath,
    We give Thee thanks, O Lord.

For the words that tell of home,
Pointing us beyond the tomb,
'Do ye this until I come,'
    We give Thee thanks, O Lord.

Till He come we take the bread,
Type of Him on whom we feed,
Him who liveth and was dead!
    We give Thee thanks, O Lord.

Till He come we take the cup;
As we at His table sup,
Eye and heart are lifted up!
    We give Thee thanks, O Lord.

For that coming, here foreshown,
For that day to man unknown,
For the glory and the throne,
    We give Thee thanks, O Lord.

THE SUPPER AND THE ADVENT.

TILL He come we own His name,
    Round His table gathering;
One in love and faith and hope,
    Waiting for an absent King.
Blessed table, where the Lord
    Sets for us His choicest cheer;
Angels have no feast like this,
    Angels wait, but sit not here.

Till He come we eat this bread,
    Seated round this heaven-spread board;
Till He come we meet and feast,
    In remembrance of the Lord.
In the banquet-house of love,
    In the Bridegroom's garden fair;
Thus we sit and feast and praise,—
    Angels look, but cannot share.

Till He come we take this cup,—
    Cup of blessing and of love;

Till He come we drink this wine,
  Emblem of the wine above,—
Emblem of the blood once shed,
  Blood of Him our sins who bare;
Angels look, but do not drink,
  Angels never taste such fare.

Till He come, beneath the shade
  Of His love we sit and sing;
Over us His banner waves,
  In His hall of banqueting.
Happy chamber, where the Lord
  Spreads the feast with viands rare;
Angels now are looking on,
  Angels serve, but cannot share.

Till He come, we wear the badge
  Of the ancient stranger-band;
Leaning on our pilgrim-staff,
  Till we reach the glorious land.
Homeless here, like Him we love,
  Watch we still in faith and prayer;
Angels have no watch like ours,
  Angels have no cross to bear.

Till He come, we fain would keep
    These our robes of earth unsoiled;
Looking for the festal dress,
    Raiment of the undefiled.
Ha! these robes of purest light,
    Fairest still among the fair!
Angels gaze, but cannot claim,—
    Angels no such raiment wear.

Till He come we keep this feast,
    Emblem of the feast above;
Marriage-supper of the Lamb,
    Festival of joy and love.
Angels hear the bridal-song,
    Angels set the festal fare:
Angels hear, but cannot join;
    Angels wait, but cannot share.

THE MASTER'S VOICE.

THE Master saith, 'My time is now at
 hand :'
We hear His words, and we at once obey.
Prepare the feast, is His divine command ;
 Thus we prepare the board, and feast with
 Him to-day.

Prepare, O Master, these dull hearts of ours
 For this Thy feast, else all in vain is spread ;
Prepare our hearts, that with new-quickened
 powers
 We may converse with Thee, and eat the
 blessed bread.

The Master saith, 'Be ready, for I come ;'
 We hear His warning voice, and we prepare.
It is a voice which bids us hasten home,
 Which bids us rise from earth to meet Him
 in the air.

THE MASTER'S VOICE.

O Master, we have heard Thy loving voice;
   Rouse our cold spirits with Thy solemn
     word:
Say, 'It is I,' and bid our souls rejoice;
   Fit us for meeting Thee, our long, long
     absent Lord.

These sounds of earth the heavenly voices
     drown,
   We scarce can hear Thee through this daily
     din:
Oh, speak in yet more penetrating tone;
   Let Thy voice reach our ears, and Thy words
     enter in.

Let discords die away, and let us hear
   The melody beyond of joy and love;
Silence the jar of earth, and let our ear
   Take in the far-off notes descending from
     above.

But not the world alone, with its rude noise,
   Absorbs the heavenly melody beyond:
The church of God, raising her angry voice,
   In the ambitious brawl drowns every holy
     sound.

THE MASTER'S VOICE.

Once Thou didst put aside the sword, and say,
   'It is enough;' oh, speak that work again:
Curb the self-will, the pride and strife allay;
   The noise of scornful words and carnal wrath restrain.

Her Babel-voices soon will silence Thine;
   Thou must withdraw, and speak to her no more.
Oh, how unlike the unity divine,
   That marked her early days,—the days of love and power!

The tempest is within her; untamed wills
   Have stirred its fury. Is the Master dumb?
To Him we cry, who the wild tempest stills;
   'Tis the fourth watch of night, and yet Thou art not come!

Carest Thou not that we are perishing?
   Awake, O Lord, speak louder than the wave:
With Thine own kingly touch the calmness bring;
   Say, Peace be still; arise, Thy broken church to save.

Let not her worldliness and strife and sin
   Provoke Thy Spirit to return no more;
And if she must be wrecked, let all within,
   Though in strange ways and diverse, find the holy shore.

---o---

HUMAN WEARINESS AND DIVINE REST.

GIVER of rest!
   This world is weary, weary in its sin.
Oh, point it to Thy home of heavenly rest,
   And bid it enter in.

Fountain of good!
   This poor world wanders, wanders sadly on;
It cries, Oh, who will show us any good?—
   Yet good it findeth none!

The good it seeks
   Is only, only to be found in Thee;
The good that fills and satisfies the heart,
   Thy love so vast and free.

Darkness is here!
   And darkness to the light the world prefers;
It stumbles on in riot and in lust,
   Its every footstep errs.

Labour is here!
   And the world seeketh rest, but findeth none.
Rest of the weary, pity its unrest;
   Oh, hear its heavy moan.

High thought is here!
   But thought is restless like the rolling waves;
It cannot cool the burning breast: oh, give
   The rest which heals and saves.

Bright love is here!
   With all the glow of its delicious smiles:
Oh, teach the sons of men the purer love,
   Love that no sin defiles.

Music is here!
   But 'tis not music with its dying falls
That soothes the broken heart, or the vexed soul
   Back to lost peace recalls.

Knowledge is here!
  And science with its fair, far-ranging sweep:
But the heart owns them not,—its void is far
  Too awful and too deep.

Laughter is here!
  But what are jests to a sin-stricken heart?
O Thou with whom the well is of calm joy,
  Thy heavenly joy impart.

True friends are here!
  But earthly friendship is a dying flower.
O deathless Friend, give friendship that will last
  The long eternal hour.

And gold is here!
  But rest was never bought with earthly gold.
Give to the weary the abiding rest,
  Which is not bought nor sold.

Glad suns are here!
  But suns, with all their brilliance, shine in
    vain;
They light not up the shaded brow of care,
  Nor banish human pain.

Sweet flowers are here!
  Flowers whose rich odours are like Eden's
    balm;
But roses cool not the heart's fever-pulse,
  Nor smooth it into calm.

Clear streams are here!
  Which in the lone high mountain-cleft have
    birth;
But these are not the waters from the throne,
  They quench no thirst of earth.

Giver of rest!
  Who restedst not when here, that we might
    rest;
Pity earth's weariness, and give, oh give
  Rest on Thy loving breast.

THE SEAMLESS RAIMENT.

If I may but touch His garment, I shall be whole.—
Matt. ix. 21.

HEM of the seamless robe,
   Through which the virtue poured;
Which told that He from whom it came
   Was earth's great King and Lord.
With tremulous eager hand,
   Thee would I touch and grasp;
No force of man nor wiles of hell
   My hand should e'er unclasp.

Hem of the seamless robe,
   Which clothed our High Priest here,
When in the lowliness of love
   He trod our earthly sphere;
When with His priestly hand
   He came and cleansed and healed;
When in the fulness of His grace
   He all that cleansing sealed.

True health, through thee, from Him
    Into this soul shall flow;
The health of heaven, the life of God
    Begun on earth below.
Instead of feebleness,
    Strength shall my portion be;
Instead of ashes, beauty then
    Shall brightly compass me.

One touch of that fair robe
    Hath all this healing given;
I need but this for blessedness,
    I need but this for heaven.
Out from its Wearer comes
    An energy divine,
Pervading with transforming power
    This tainted soul of mine.

Who touches it is free!
    His chains are snapt in twain;
Immortal purity is his,
    Instead of mortal stain.
Through it flows priestly power
    To liberate the soul;
It purges sin, it casts out ill,
    It makes the bruisèd whole.

Through it pours royal strength,
    The endless life to give;
It wakes the sleeper from his sleep,
    It bids the dead man live.
This priestly-royal robe,
    The robe without a seam,
Has wrought strange miracles on earth,
    Beyond the dreamer's dream.

Thrown o'er the soul, it works
    To quicken and to save;
Thrown o'er the tomb-enshrouded dust,
    It disenchants the grave.
Thrown over this sad earth,
    As yet its folds shall be,
It shall wipe out the wasting curse,
    And bid corruption flee.

Ages of sickness then
    Shall in a moment go;
The age of everlasting health
    Shall be begun below.
Ages of darkness end;
    Light, with its fair array,
Long veiled within the seamless robe,
    Shall burst forth into day.

CREATION'S SONG.

> Te cuncta nempe prædicant;
> Te terra, pontus, sidera
> Cantu celebrant æmulo;
>   Peccator unus dissonat.
> OLD HYMN.

DEEP calleth unto deep,
  Jehovah He is God!
Stream answereth to stream,
  And spreads His praise abroad.

Star calleth unto star,
  Jehovah He is God!
Each rising sun and moon
  Spreadeth His praise abroad.

Heaven calleth unto earth,
  Jehovah He is God!
Earth calleth unto heaven,
  And spreads His praise abroad.

In the great song we join,
    Jehovah He is God!
  We echo the great voice,
    And spread His praise abroad.

———o———

ONE FAITH AND HOPE.

ONLY one cross!
  And to that cross He leadeth all His own.
They gather round it, and its healing falls
  Upon each sickly one.

Only one fold!
  And to that fold the Shepherd brings His sheep;
On the green pastures there, to feed them all,
  And with His staff to keep.

Only one way!
  One way for all the many wanderers;
Returning from a thousand various parts,
  Through earth's long stormy years.

Only one city!
  And to that city His beloved come;
Brought by Himself to find in it for ever
  Their safe and blessed home.

Only one Christ!
  And to that Christ the Father draws each
    eye,
Bidding them look, and in that looking live,
  That they no more may die.

Only one heaven!
  Into whose glory He His own doth call;
Where all is sinless, sorrowless, and bright,—
  Where Christ is all in all.

THE EYE OPENING ON THE CROSS.

FOR the first time I see
    The glory of the cross; how dark before!
Thanks to the mighty hand that swept away the mist,
    And from before my eyes the veil so kindly tore.

The Son of God is there,
    The holy One is hanging on that tree.
He took on Him, in love, my sins, and bore them all:
    The Just for the unjust has paid the penalty.

My Surety hangeth there,
    My Substitute, who gave His life for mine;
Who died my death that I should live; transferring all
    My guilt to Him, to me His excellence divine.

He died my awful death;
  Therefore I know that I shall never die;
And from that death divine, to me, flows righteous love,
  The love that cannot change, the love of God most high.

How brightly now that cross
  Shineth; in splendour like a new-made sun!
All light is there; no gloom, no terror, and no wrath;
  The grace that floweth out has heights and depths unknown.

That cross,—it suits me well:
  It soothes my fears, and speaks true words of peace;
It breaks my bonds in twain, and liberates my soul;
  It healeth all my wounds, and bids my sorrows cease.

It gives me heavenly strength,
  And in that strength I fight the fight of God;

It draws me on; it lifts me up from sin and
 dust;
 It lightens all my path, and shows the
 heavenly road.

It giveth peace with God!
 It gives the peace of God that passeth
 thought;
It shows the Christ of God, Himself our only
 peace,—
The sure and perfect peace, which the world
 knoweth not.

At morn and even it shines!
 It is our matin and our vesper song.
Like Israel's desert cloud, it will abide with us;
 'Twill cheer our earthly path, however rough
 and long.

It is our resting-place,
 Where we behold the piercèd hands and
 side,
And where the wondrous cry, ''Tis finished!'
 we can hear:
 There safe as in the rock of God we would
 abide.

It is our meeting-place,
  Where righteousness and grace have met in love;
Where God the holy can unholy man embrace,
  Where earth saluteth heaven descending from above.

No cross of gold or gems,
  Graven to adorn, by man's device and art,
Is that in which my soul delights and ever trusts,—
  With which, in guilt's dread hour, I calm my trembling heart.

The all-atoning death,
  In shame and agony for sinners here.
The finished work of love, the reconciling blood,—
  That is the cross which in my heart of hearts I wear.

I need no earthly cross,
  No carnal emblem of a dying Lord;

It seemeth but to mock His shame, and
    blood, and cries :
  With closèd eyes I muse upon the awful
    word,—

Awful, yet blessed still,—
  'TIS FINISHED, the atoning work is done!
All righteousness fulfilled, all shadows passed
    away ;
  Shines now all clear and fair the one un-
    setting sun.

I glory in the cross!
  There with the Son of God the death I
    died.
By it this evil world is crucified to me,
  And I unto this evil world am crucified.

O Christ the Son of God!
  Reveal Thyself to me, Thy truth and grace,
That I, partaking of Thy fulness daily here,
  May, when Thy kingdom comes, behold
    Thy glorious face.

EARLY SAVED.

Ὃν γὰρ φιλεῖ Θεὸς γ' ἀποθνήσκει νέος.
OLD GREEK FRAGMENT.

O EARLY saved!
  Gone to thy resting-place,
Without the fight or race,
Without the toil or sweat,
The burden and the fret,
The sorrow and the sin,
The bitter war within,
Without the daily strife
Of this tempestuous life!

Only in dreams since then,
  Only in dreams we've met:
Brief meeting and quick parting this;
  Yet can we e'er forget
The short but blessed past,
  The days of childhood's love,
Cut short in sweetest prime,
  To be resumed above?

O early saved, not lost!
　　Life and not death is thine:
Not wrecked, but landed safely on the
　　coast
　　Where suns for ever shine.
Born not to die, but live,
　　Thy life is now begun.
Born not for storm, but calm,
　　Thy haven is now won.
Born not for night, but day,
　　For ever shines thy sun.
Born not for earth, but heaven,
　　Thy one brief hour is done.
All now with thee is well,
　　Thou thrice-beloved one:
We meet thee in the land
　　Where sorrow is unknown;
To sit with thee in light
　　Upon the eternal throne!

TO THE HOLY SPIRIT.

> Te docente discitur,
> Ostendente cernitur,
> Conferente capitur,
> Donum sapientiæ.—OLD HYMN.

HOLY Spirit, spring of gladness,
    Into glory turn this gloom ;
Make a morning of this midnight,
    Make a temple of this tomb.

Into summer turn this winter,
    Soothe this tempest into calm ;
Out of wretched dust and ashes
    Bring the beauty and the balm.

Into freedom turn this bondage,
    Into laughter turn these tears ;
Give me heavenly health for sickness,
    Joy and song for sighs and tears.

Wake, O north wind, freshly stirring,
   Blow upon a drooping earth;
Come, thou south wind, to my garden,
   That the spices may flow forth.

Teach us, O Thou blessed Teacher!
   With Thy teaching all is plain;
Give the everlasting wisdom,
   Without which all here is vain.

Keep from falsehood, save from folly;
   Give the real and the true;
Pour in truth in days of error,
   Freshen us with heavenly dew.

With the words of peace and comfort
   Enter each sad heart and home;
With Thy balm of consolation,
   Mighty Comforter, oh come!

Are we not Thy living temples,
   Honoured once, and loved so well?
Visit us with sevenfold fulness,
   Here in all Thy glory dwell.

Shall the altar-fire be scattered?
   Shall the incense cease to burn?
Shall Thy temple be forsaken?
   Wilt Thou not to us return?

———o———

OTHER GODS.

UNSTABLE age!
   Hither and thither tossed;
Still chasing what is new,
   In mists and mazes lost.

Unanchored barque!
   Drifting across the deep,
Without a helm or chart
   The onward course to keep.

Thy men of thought,
   Thy heroes of the mind,
Are like the driven leaves,—
   Reeds shaken with the wind.

'Tis self-will all!
   And 'Ye shall be as gods'
Is still the tempting bait
   That deadly ill forebodes;—

Dark unbelief,
   Belief of the dark lie,—
The first lie and the last,
   'Ye shall not surely die.'

No Christ, no God!
   This is the gloomy goal
In which man's progress ends,—
   The chaos of the soul!

No book of heaven
   We need to lead us on;
Man is his own best guide,
   And science is his sun!

Back to the gods
   Of Greece and Rome again;
So graceful, glad, and fair,—
   These be thy gods, O men!

Back to the groves
  Of palm-fringed Lebanon,
Where Syrian Ashtaroth
  Bent o'er Endymion.

To Ida come,
  With wine and wreaths and odes,
Upon Olympus stand,
  And worship Homer's gods!

Seek Delos now,
  Poseidon's island green,
Where knelt Ionian maids
  To Artemis their queen.

Worship the earth,
  The sky, the streams, the sod;
Worship the winds and waves;
  But not the Christ of God!

Come, worship power,
  Beauty, and love, and soul;
But not the living God,
  Who made this mighty whole!

Bow down to self,
    Take nature to thy heart;
Say earth is God, and God
    Is of this earth a part!

Yet God is God!
    And man a wrinkled leaf,
Tossed o'er these hills and vales
    By winds of joy and grief.

God will be God!
    The day is coming fast
When He shall claim His due,—
    Jehovah, First and Last.

He speaks, and earth
    Shrinks from His voice of dread;
He summons man, but man
    Is dumb and hides his head.

He speaks again!
    But from His face they flee;
The cry of agony
    Is, Mountains, cover me!

He speaks again!
    They gather round the throne;
Their boasts are at an end,
    Their mockery is done.

He calls aloud!
    He lifts the iron rod;
His foes are crushed; and earth
    Now owns the living God.

The idols fall!
    The idol-shrines are gone;
Ye gods of lust and hate,
    Your reign on earth is done!

The fool no more
    Utters the atheist lie;
The scoffer's voice is dumb,
    And mute his blasphemy.

THE WINTER IS PAST.

AGE of the ages,
    Whence comest thou?
Laurel and olive
    Shading thy brow.

Age of the peaceful,
    Joy in thy train;
Age of the holy,
    Welcome again!

Age of the iron,
    Vanish your years;
Age of the golden
    Now reappears.

Love in its gladness
    Shines from above;
Peace in its pureness
    Comes with the love.

Light of the holy
    Covers the earth;
Life of the blessed
    Springs into birth.

Sword of the spoiler,
    Sheathe thee at last;
Hosts are disbanding,
    Havoc is past.

Flag of the mighty,
    Lower thy star;
Idle thy flaunting,
    Silent the war.

Tower of the watchman,
    Needed no more,
Level thy bulwarks,
    Agèd and hoar.

Bar, gate, and rampart,
    Sink in the dust;
Helmet and buckler,
    Moulder and rust.

Shout of the victor
 O'er the oppressed;
Wail of the vanquished,
 Be now at rest!

Sigh of the captive,
 Sink into peace;
Song of the warrior,
 Now thou shalt cease.

Roar of the breaker,
 Melt into calm;
Gale of the desert,
 Breathe into balm.

Wail of the shipwreck,
 Rise thou no more;
Silent the tempest,
 Tranquil the shore.

Palm of the moonlight,
 Wave thou above;
Tell of the triumph,
 Speak of the love.

Roses of Sharon,
  Muster your flowers;
Snow of the myrtle,
  Whiten our bowers.

Bloom of the almond,
  Gladden our spring;
Scent of the citron,
  Sweet odour fling.

Dew of the morning,
  Scatter your gold;
Dew of the evening,
  Splendour unfold.

Song of the song-bird,
  Send out your strain;
Voice of the turtle,
  Steal o'er the plain.

Summer-bright beauty
  Maketh earth fair;
Summer-sweet fragrance
  Filleth the air.

Summer-green verdure
   Smiles o'er the plain;
Summer-glad radiance
   Shines o'er the main.

Past is earth's winter,
   Bright is its May;
Rise up, my fair one,
   Haste, come away.

Daughter of Zion,
   Sorrow no more;
Light is arising,
   Darkness is o'er.

Shame is forgotten,
   Exile is past;
Beauty for ashes
   Cometh at last.

Lebanon's glory
   Riseth to view;
Carmel and Sharon
   Flourish anew.

FAITH AND HOPE.

ON both sides is my anchor firmly cast;
    Before, behind, my faith looks stedfastly.
There is no darkness in that long, long past,
    And in that future no uncertainty.

'Mid the unseen it rests, and finds all sure,
    The unseen past contains my spirit's peace;
The unseen future, ever to endure,
    Contains my consolation and my bliss.

The cross is peace, and that sums up the past;
    The crown is joy, and that my future sums:
I need but simpler faith, faith that shall last,
    The hope that liberates and overcomes.

Thus 'mid the silent and unseen I dwell;
    The near and visible are not my home.
My soul goes out to the invisible,
    The things that have been, and are yet to come.

These are the true and real, the good and fair;
  These are our solace in life's heaviest woes:
The heights and depths of peace and rest are there,
  And there the spirit finds its true repose.

———o———

I AM WITH THEE.

'TIS a dead world through which I walk;
  My Life, oh, still with me abide!
Each hour impart Thy life anew;
  My Life, leave not my side!

Within, without, deep darkness reigns;
  My Light, my Light, be ever near!
If thou shouldst leave me, all is dark;
  My Light, oh stay to cheer!

The storm is round me and above;
  O calmer of the tempest, come!
Soothe the strong blast,—too strong for me;
  Or take me, take me home!

Deep are the waters, fierce the flame;
    Be with me both in fire and wave!
Let them not seize me nor o'erwhelm,
    In trial's hour me save!

Before me lies a path unknown,
    It may be tears, and pain, and death:
Oh, speak the word which cheers and nerves,
    'Fight the good fight of faith.'

Take Thou my hand, my Guide, my Guide!
    My eager hand I stretch to Thee:
Hold Thou me up, lead Thou me on,
    All shall be well with me.

THE DROPS OF THE NIGHT.

Song of Sol. v. 2.

OUT in the dew and cold He stands,
　　The drops of night are on His hair:
In patient love He waits without;
　　And who, who keeps Him there?

All heaven is in His earnest voice,
　　All glory on His brow so fair:
In sorrowing love He stands without;
　　And who, who keeps Him there?

'Open to me, beloved one,
　　With me thy heart and dwelling share:'
But still at the barred door He stands;
　　And who, who keeps Him there?

He hath no place to lay His head,
　　No one a home or roof will spare:
No one respondeth when He knocks;
　　And who, who keeps Him there?

The winds are out, the storm is up,
    Freezing and sharp the midnight air:
He does not leave, but knocketh on;
    And who, who keeps Him there?

Our ear is sealed, our heart is cold,
    And we refuse both hearth and fare:
He speaks, we hear not: Ah, 'tis we,
    Yes, we who keep Him there.

But now no more we shut Thee out,
    O Thou, the fairest of the fair:
Come in, Thou blessed One; we will
    No longer keep Thee there.

He cometh in, my board I spread,
    My wine and viands I prepare:
The night-drops fall, the night-winds blow;
    He is no longer there.

He sups with me, and I with Him,
    I wipe the night-drops from His hair:
I hear no more His knock without;
    He is no longer there.

WHO IS HE THAT CONDEMNETH?

IN the death of Christ I die;
    In the life of Christ I live!
All my ill He from me takes,
    All His good to me doth give.

With Him nailèd to the cross,
    With Him buried in the grave,
With Him raised from bonds and death,
    Life for ever thus I have.

He the fight for me hath fought,
    And for me the battle won;
Thus in weakness I am made
    Victor through the conquering One.

He the guilt for me hath borne,
    Condemnation now is done:
Wrath has vanished; I am made
    Righteous in the righteous One.

On me love for ever rests;
  Like a river peace doth flow:
Christ the mighty work hath done;
  God is for me, this I know.

His name now is one with mine,
  I in Him, and He in me;
On His breastplate is my name,
  Priest and Advocate is He.

Covered with Thy robe, O Christ,
  All Thy beauty now is mine;
Me in Thee the Judge beholds,
  My life now is lost in Thine.

Since Thou livest, I shall live;
  Never canst Thou me disown.
Not the cross for me remains,
  Nor the manger, but the crown.

TOWARD THE MARK.

MY tempted soul, arise and fight!
   Round thee are perils of the night.
Sleep not, but rouse thee for the war,
Nor shrink from pain, and wound, and scar.

Do snares lie all thy path along?
And are these spells for thee too strong?
   Up then, and grasp the hand divine,
   Take that almighty hand in thine.

Does conscious weakness cast thee down?
What! dost thou think thyself alone?
   Know'st thou not One who by thy side
   Doth ever stand, whate'er betide?

Know'st thou not Him who saith to thee,
Be strong, weak soul, be strong in me,—
   Who gives thee His almighty power,
   To strengthen thee in peril's hour?

His is an arm that cannot fail,
Whatever foe may thee assail:
　His is a love that changes not;
　Trust Him, thou shalt not be forgot.

O weary feet! the day of rest
Is coming, when, no more oppressed
　With storm or toil or smiting sun,
　We shall take rest, all labour done.

O heavy eyes! look up, look up;
See far above thee the bright hope!
　Look through the mist, and see beyond
　The fairest day that ever dawned.

Be still, be still, my throbbing heart,
The strong One will His strength impart;
　Firm clasp His hand who claspeth thine,
　No power shall e'er that clasp untwine.

In calmest day or roughest night,
Still lean upon His loving might;
　He knows alike thy joy and woe,
　And will He let His loved one go?

THE ETERNAL ROCK.

UPON the Rock I plant my foot!
   Amid time's shifting, sinking sands,
Amid the hurricanes of life,
   Fixed and immoveable it stands.

All else is moving; it alone
   Shakes not, nor yields, nor crumbles down:
Time and its tempests it defies;
   Changes to it are things unknown.

It grows not old, it turns not grey;
   It boldly baffles every shock:
Repelling earth, defying hell,
   It standeth firm, the eternal Rock.

The earthquakes of the ages strike
   Against it with increasing rage;
It trembles not, nor shrinks in fear
   From the dark warfare of the age.

It lifts its head above the clouds,
    It braves the wrath and scorn of foes;
Deep as the everlasting hills,
    It strikes its roots in still repose.

Rock of eternity, amid
    All changes here, I rest on Thee!
Rock of the ages that are past,
    Rock of the ages yet to be.

LORD, INCREASE OUR FAITH.

MY past, O Lord, with all its scenes
    Of varying good and ill,
Of sorrow and of joy, has been
    The unfolding of Thy will.

My future, with its changing scenes
    Of light and shadow sown,
Is in Thy hands, O God of love,
    Though now to me unknown.

Keep me from planning brighter days,
    Save me from care and pride;
Give what Thy wisdom deemeth right,
    And I am satisfied.

A fuller, warmer heart of love,
    Give, gracious Lord, to me,—
A simpler, stronger, nobler faith,
    And happier thoughts of Thee.

CHRISTMAS CHEER.

REJOICE, my soul, the Christ has come!
    With all thy powers arise and sing.
To earth He comes in lowly love,
    The manger has received the King.

O'er Bethlehem the glory rests,
    And from that glory bursts the song
Of angels, which the wondering earth
    Through all its ages shall prolong.

The Son becomes the servant here,
    From this to us all glory springs;
Lower than angels God is made,—
    That infant is the King of kings!

The Lamb of sacrifice lies here,
    Preparing for the altar-fire;
True Lamb of God, without a spot,—
    He of all nations the desire.

O long, long promised, come at last,
   In human weakness man to save;
Thy lifetime's work for us to do,
   Even from the cradle to the grave.

God, in His lowliness of love,
   From highest heaven to earth hath come;
Though rich, for us becoming poor,
   Despising not the Virgin's womb.

Despising not the manger-bed,
   He takes on earth the lowest place;
To poverty bows down, that we
   May taste the fulness of His grace.

O grace of Christ, how full and sweet!
   O love of God, how rich and free!
The Father's well-beloved Son
   Hath stooped to shame and woe for me!

O stony manger of the inn!
   Poor casket thou for such a gem:
On thee we gaze, in thee we find
   Heaven's glory, earth's bright diadem.

IT WON'T BE LONG.

BROTHERS, wherefore fear ye?
    Onwards, forwards steer ye;
See the green shore near ye.

Kindly winds are blowing,
Homewards we are going,
Slack not in your rowing.

Soon shall be the meeting,
Sweet shall be the greeting,
Hours are swiftly fleeting.

Hark! the voice of cheering,
As the shore is nearing,
Press along unfearing.

COME TO THY TEMPLE.

GREAT Lord and Master of the temple, come!
O visit in Thy holy love Thy shrine.
How much of worldly vanity dwells here,
  In that which should have been unearthly and divine!

False gods are here, and idols all around,
  With idol-altars smoking everywhere;
The fumes of idol-incense rise and spread
  Their odours in the once all still and hallowed air.

The world is here, with laughter and with song,
  With dance and gaiety and idle jest;
Here where Thy name was named; of which
    Thou saidst,
  Here will I ever dwell, this is my place of rest.

O holy home of God, where all things calm,
  Pure, and unworldly should alone be found;
O church of God, how unlike what thou wert!
  Unclean and common now the consecrated
    ground!

Knit into one Thy living members, Lord;
  Purge Thy one temple of all things unclean:
Silence the din, and strife, and angry jar;
  Give unity and peace; cast out the wrath
    and sin.

Cast out the buyers and the sellers, Lord;
  Let not the world pollute the hallowed fane.
Oh, make Thy church what it shall one day be,
  Like her great Head above, without a spot
    or stain.

Let the sweet incense from her altars rise,
  Let the pure sacrifice to Thee be given;
Clothe Thou her priests with truth and holiness,
  And let the songs of earth resemble those
    of heaven.

Strip off all unreality and pride;
   Give Thou the broken and the contrite heart;
Descend and dwell in these polluted shrines,
   And let Thy Spirit all His heavenly grace
      impart.

Let not her worldliness, and strife, and sin,
   So banish Thee that Thou return no more;
Or if she must be wrecked, let all within,
   Though in strange ways and diverse, reach
      the holy shore.

PENTECOST.

THE Master hath His word fulfilled;
  And though we still are far from home,
The days of orphanage are past,—
  The Comforter has come!

The promise of the Father now
  Descends; our lips no more are dumb:
The rushing mighty wind is heard,—
  The Comforter has come!

The true Enlightener of the dark,
  Of heavenly gifts the soul and sum,
The mighty Quickener of the dead,—
  The Comforter has come!

The Breath from the four winds of heaven,
  That breathes into the awful tomb,
The resurrection-breath of God,—
  The Comforter has come!

Midnight has blossomed into morn,
   For gladness we exchange our gloom;
The joy unspeakable is ours,—
   The Comforter has come!

Our fetters break, our burdens fall,
   Fresh rays from heaven our souls illume;
Our prison-bars lie broken round,—
   The Comforter has come!

Now are we strong for service high,
   For toil, or pain, or martyrdom;
Now we can face the sword or fire,—
   The Comforter has come!

Now are we nerved for holy fight,
   For longer life or earlier doom;
Our helmet, shield, and sword are on,—
   The Comforter has come!

The fire from heaven descends in power,
   Our dross for ever to consume;
In holy liberty we walk,—
   The Comforter has come!

The south wind blows, the kindly sun
  Ripens our garden's summer-bloom,
And hangs the fruit upon our boughs,—
  The Comforter has come!

———o———

THE CROSS-WEARER.

I AM crucified with Christ,
  With Him nailed upon the tree:
Not THE cross, then, do I bear;
  But the cross it beareth me.
Solemn cross on which I died,
One with Him the crucified.

Shall I take that blood-stained cross,
  Cross of agony and shame,
Cross of Him who fought my fight,
  Cross of Him who overcame,—
Shall I deck myself with thee,
Awful cross of Calvary?

Shall I drag thee through the crowd,
  'Mid the laughter that is there;
Whirl thee through the giddy waltz
  Bound upon my neck or hair?
Awful cross of Calvary,
Shall I deck myself with thee?

Shall I make that lowly cross
  Minister of woman's pride?
Drawing eyes to me that should
  Fix upon the Crucified?
Awful cross of Calvary,
Shall I deck myself with thee?

Shall I call this glittering gem,
  Made for show and vanity,
Shall I call this gaud a cross,—
  Cross of Him who died for me?
Shall I deck myself with thee,
Awful cross of Calvary?

Cross of man's device, I turn
  From thee to Himself, my Lord;
What can this symbolic gem
  Do for me;—what peace afford?

Shall I deck myself with thee,
Awful cross of Calvary?

I am crucified with Christ;
　Yet I live through Him who died:
Shall that cross of blood and woe
　Minister to human pride?
Shall I deck myself with thee,
Awful cross of Calvary?

THOU SHALT KNOW HEREAFTER.

IS good or evil reigning here,
    One lord or many bearing sway?
Who is the ruler of this sphere?
    So ask we oft,—but who shall say?
Sin triumphs, death and pain are rife,
    The best and worst like sorrows know;
All is disorder, darkness, strife:
    Who, then, is master here below?
Whence has this chaos come, and how
    Or when shall earth shake off this load?
One is the word, to which we bow,
    'Be still, and know that I am God.'

Unequal seem all things, unjust;
    Toil, tears, a wilderness of crime:
Dark passions, deadly hate, foul lust,
    Fill up the chronicles of time.
And yet each murmur we repel,
    What we now know not we shall know:
Let us be patient; all is well,
    For history is stern and slow.

Let us be patient; God is wise;
  He does not fling His gold abroad;
Each plan profound our patience tries:
  'Be still, and know that I am God.'

Let us be patient; God is love;
  All wrong shall yet be righted here:
The bitterest shall the sweetest prove;
  The dark and tangled all be clear.
The worst shall then appear the best,
  And from confusion order spring;
The wisdom then shall stand confessed,
  And power of the Eternal King.
Trust Him, He knows our troubled state;
  He knows each winding of the road:
Let us sit calmly down and wait;
  'Be still, and know that I am God.'

THE COMING CREED.

THE creeds have gone, so speaks the age;
    The era of the sects is past.
Forward! In spite of saint or sage,
    True freedom has begun at last.

The Christ of God is now no more,
    The Christ of man now sits supreme;
The cross is part of mythic lore,
    The resurrection-morn a dream.

The age's progress fears no God,
    No righteous law, no Judge's throne;
Man bounds along his new-found road,
    And calls this universe his own.

Not faith in God, but faith in man,
    Is pilot now, and sail, and oar:
The creeds are shrivelled, cold, and wan;
    The Christ that has been is no more!

Old truth, which once struck deep in hearts,
  Fights hard for life, but fights in vain ;
Old error into vigour starts,
  And fable comes to life again.

Old misbelief becomes earth's creed ;
  The falsehood lives, the truth has died :
Man leans upon a broken reed,
  And falls in helplessness of pride.

He spurns the hand that would have led,
  The lips that would have spoken love ;
The Book that would his soul have fed,
  And taught the wisdom from above.

The ever-standing cross, to him
  Is but a Hebrew relic vain ;
The wondrous birth at Bethlehem
  A fiction of the wandering brain.

He wants no Saviour and no light ;
  No teacher but himself he needs :
He knows not of a human night,
  Save from the darkness of the creeds.

Eternal Light, hide not Thy face;
  Eternal Truth, direct our way;
Eternal Love, shine forth in grace,
  Reveal *our* darkness and *Thy* day!

―――o―――

THE YOKE OF THE TRUE MASTER.

THY yoke! All other yokes are hard,
  But Thine is soft and light;
It fills the soul that puts it on
  With an unknown delight.

Thy yoke! There are no chains in it;
  It giveth eagle's wings:
The soul that takes it hastens on,
  And, as he goeth, sings.

Thy burden is a load of love,
  And love makes all things sweet;
It gives fresh vigour to the frame,
  New swiftness to the feet.

It does not stay us in our course,
  Nor make our service hard;
It cheers us on, and points us to
  The day of glad reward.

Oh, give us then Thy pleasant yoke,
  Thy blessed burden lay
On us, that we may do Thy work
  In our brief service-day.

Help us, O Lord, to serve Thee well
  In weakness here below;
That we, rejoicing in Thy love,
  Our love to Thee may show.

The service that we render now,
  'Mid conflict, grief, and fear,
Is such as angels cannot give
  In their all-peaceful sphere;—

Service which ceases when we part
  With foes, and sins, and pain,—
Service that glorifies Thy name
  Beyond all service then.

Right gladly then we take the yoke,
  And bear it hour by hour;
We glory in that service here
  Which magnifies Thy power.

Sustain us here, most gracious Lord!
  Quicken our love and faith,
That we may serve Thee well, and be
  Still faithful unto death.

BE STRONG.

IN God, your God, be strong,
　　His power and grace are thine;
The battle is the battle of thy God,
　　The victory is divine.

True warriors of the King,
　　Fear not the mighty host
Of powers and principalities beneath;
　　Heed not the hellish boast.

Dread not the evil day,
　　Dark as that day may be.
Courage! However mighty is thy foe,
　　A greater is with thee!

Take up, ye men of war,
　　The armour of the Lord;
The panoply of heaven, the spear-proof
　　shield,
　　The helmet, and the sword.

Quit you like men of might;
  Be strong, and face the foe:
War the good warfare here of faith and
    truth,
  Lay the great tempter low.

To him who overcomes
  Does the bright crown belong;
His is the everlasting recompense,
  The victor's palm and song.

BEYOND THE MISTS.

THINNER and thinner grows the veil
    Between us and the heaven of God;
The mists are clearing from the dale,
    Comes the last winding of the road.

Years hurry past, and earth grows old,
    And time's sad sea is ebbing dry;
Long-covered hills their heads unfold,
    The distant has become the nigh.

Round us the darknesses still grow,
    But brighter burn the lights above;
Earth's lamps are waxing dim and low,
    As onward through its wastes we move.

Our earthly treasures lessen fast;
    Larger our heavenly stores become:
Earth like a waste becomes at last,
    And heaven more truly seems our home.

They go; we weep, yet dry our tears:
    They die, yet die not; all is well:
They leave but feebleness and fears,
    In immortality to dwell.

'Farewell!' we say. Why speak we thus?
    Is it not 'well' for ever there?
'Tis *they* should say 'Farewell' to us,
    Still compassed here with sin and care.

They enter in, we mark the road;
    We follow with our eyes afar,
Like one who watches, as some cloud
    Blots from our view some long-loved star.

Nearer now seems the land unseen,
    And nearer too the glorious day,
When the thin veil, now drawn between,
    Shall vanish into light away.

Meanwhile the little flock remains,
    And Israel's Shepherd keeps the fold;
Safe, while His arm this earth sustains
    Under His shadow as of old.

And one by one He calls them up,
　　Out from the peril and the war;
Above the fear, above the hope,
　　Beyond the tumult and the jar.

---o---

ELIJAH'S ASCENSION.

ON his Lord's bosom now
　　He resteth from his toil:
Done is his fiery warfare here,
　　Purged of all earthly soil.

The fiery chariot comes;
　　He knoweth well for whom:
It halts, he enters it, and goes
　　In awful splendour home.

At Jordan's margin green
　　He lays his burden down,
Shakes off mortality, and mounts
　　To his eternal crown.

He does not stay to doff
   The well-worn mantle here;
Just as he is he passes up,
   Without a care or fear.

All travel-stained his feet,
   His sandals soiled and torn;
His raiment rough, and strange, and old,
   With life's sore journey worn.

With weary limbs that day,
   On farewell errands bound,
Bethel's rough hills he climbed, then sought
   The river-plain renowned;—

The plain where Israel's camp
   First stood on Canaan's shore;
The pillar-glory overhead,
   Marching in light before.

Smiting the water's strength,
   He parts the flood in twain,
Moves o'er its dark uncovered bed,
   Not to return again.

Here, where of old the Lord
  In wondrous grace came down
To lay His honoured saint to rest
  Deep in a grave unknown,—

Here He descends again,
  In fiery chariot driven,
To snatch from death His prophet-saint,
  And bear him up to heaven.

Far above Nebo's height
  He moves triumphant on;
From higher peaks than Pisgah's, sees
  That goodly Lebanon.

All the fair land he leaves,
  Beneath his feet now lies;
And Salem in her zone of hills
  Looks up to see him rise.

His mighty works are done;
  These flaming coursers bear
This over-wearied son of toil
  Beyond both hope and fear.

He needs no armour now,
   No buckler for his breast;
His fight is fought, his victory won,
   He rests where warriors rest.

But now he heard the noise
   Of Jordan's turbid roar;
Next moment he is by the fount
   Where living waters pour.

Fair are the palms he left
   Behind him as he rose;
But fairer far the palms which shade
   Life's river as it flows.

Fair is Samaria's hill,
   Bright is its crown of pride;
More fair the city where *she* dwells,—
   The Lamb's immortal Bride.

There, in his Father's house,
   The pilgrim rests at last,
His Cherith-days, his Horeb-nights
   Of pilgrimage all past.

No more he wars with kings,
  Or fights with sin and wrong;
His are the crown and palm and harp,
  And his the endless song.

---o---

THE STILL SMALL VOICE.

KEEP silence, God is speaking,
  Hear thou His voice;
He speaks in loving-kindness,—
  Listen, rejoice.

Aside from human converse,
  Come thou alone;
Be ready still to welcome
  His stillest tone.

Thy God, O man, but wanteth
  Thy ready ear.
He knoweth what thou needest:
  Be still, and hear.

He loves to speak,—O listen!
    Turn not away.
His heart to thee is beating;
    Stay, trifler, stay!

That which He speaks is gladness,
    No word to grieve.
His words are words of healing,
    Hear, then, and live.

He draweth near in mercy;
    He loves to spare:
His hand on us He layeth,—
    All heaven is there.

The years that seem the darkest
    Are years of love:
He speaketh through the darkness
    Peace from above.

The days that seem all sunless
    Are days of light;
For God Himself is in them
    To make all bright.

The hours of pain and weakness
  Are hours of strength.
The health seems long in coming;
  It comes at length.

He comes when waves are tossing,
  In storm and shade.
With 'It is I' He cometh;
  'Be not afraid!'

---o---

FOR ME.

HE must increase, and I decrease:
  Less of myself and more of Him!
I am all emptiness, and He
  A fountain filled up to the brim.

He takes my poverty and want,
  To give me His o'erflowing wealth;
He takes my sickness on Himself,
  To give me His celestial health.

He goeth down that I may rise,
   Is bound in chains to set me free;
Enters my lonely prison-house,
   That I may know His liberty.

He drinks my sorrow, weeps my tears,
   That I may taste His joy and rest;
His hunger and His thirst are mine,
   That mine may be His heavenly feast.

He takes my name, and gives me His,
   For my poor raiment gives His own;
And all that He has done is mine,—
   His worth, His fulness, and His crown.

KNOW YE NOT?

WHAT! Know ye not
    That, of all those who run some
        earthly race,
  Only one wins the prize?
So run that ye may win;
End well, end well what ye begin.
Lest turning back ye fall,
And end by losing all,—
  O loss without repair!

What! Know ye not
  That the true temple of the Lord are ye,
    Home of the Holy Ghost?
Defile, destroy it not,
But keep it, keep it without spot.
It is no earthly shrine,
But heavenly and divine,—
  Pollute ye not its courts!

What! Know ye not
  That saints shall judge the world, nay, angels
     too?
  Judge then true judgment here,—
Walking in ways upright,
As judges of the age of light,
With holy charity,
Yet with calm equity,
  Doing and speaking truth.

What! Know ye not
  That the unrighteous cannot enter in,
    Nor tread the holy ground?
The imperfect is not there,
But beauty, beauty everywhere,
Perfection near and far;
No taint, nor sin, nor jar,—
  All holiness and peace!

What! Know ye not
  That they who love the world have not in
    them
  The love of God? That love
Comes from a holy heaven,
And to us here on earth is given,

To draw us up from earth,
To where it has its birth,
   The bosom of our God.

What! Know ye not
  That thus even here ye must be holy men?
    The Nazarites of God;
That walk with the unseen,
With feet washed in the laver clean,
And garments undefiled.
Though all around be soiled,
   Thou must be pure and fair.

LINGER NOT.

THE time is short!
   If thou wouldst work for God, it must
      be now,—
  If thou wouldst win the garland for thy
     brow,—
Redeem the time.

Shake off earth's sloth!
   Go forth with staff in hand while yet 'tis
     day,
   Set out with girded loins upon thy way,—
Up, linger not!

Fold not thy hands!
   What has the pilgrim of the cross and
     crown
   To do with luxury or couch of down?—
On, pilgrim, on!

LINGER NOT.

Sheathe not the sword!
   The battle lies before thee, and the prize
   Hangs yonder, far above these earthly skies;
Fight the good fight!

Life ebbs apace!
   Fast crumbles down this house of mortal clay;
   Fling not, like dust, thy precious hours away:
The end is near.

Faint not, O man!
   Follow the Master through the noble strife,
   Pursue His footsteps till they end in life:
Be strong in Him.

With His reward
   He comes, He tarries not, His day is near;
   When men least look for Him will He be here:
Prepare for Him.

Let not the flood
   Sweep thy firm feet from the eternal rock;
   Face calmly, solemnly, the billow's shock;
Nor fear the storm.

Withstand the foe;
  Die daily, that for ever thou mayst live:
  Be faithful unto death; thy Lord will give
The crown of life.

———o———

THE STRENGTH OF EVIL.

IN this great world of ours
    Nothing is small or poor;
For each hour's smallest thing is knit
    To the long evermore.

The common deed or word,
    Of which we took no heed,
Ends in a vast eternity,
    As in the tree the seed.

No room to trifle here;
    To jest away life's hours,
As if we were but born to laugh,
    And sport among the flowers.

THE STRENGTH OF EVIL.

Sin spreadeth round and round
   In all we hear or see;
Each drop enough to poison earth
   And stain eternity.

Its lightest touch is death;
   And from each spark there come
Fires, through the ages spreading wide,
   The harbingers of doom.

The soul that sinneth dies!
   He who has swerved aside
From the full-hearted love of God,
   He has already died.

The sentence has gone forth
   From the great Judge of all,
In whose high estimate of guilt
   No sin of man is small.

O endless fruit of sin!
   O solemn doom of God!
One drop of evil upon earth
   Swells to a world-wide flood.

One sin sweeps over time,
   Rushing through silent space,
Like a dark angel, to destroy
   The new-created race.

Yet as the one sad sin
   Brought death, and woe, and strife,
So the one righteousness has brought
   The everlasting life.

TRANSFORMED DARKNESS.

LET me call nothing dark or ill,
    In which the name of God I find;
Let me call nothing bright or good,
    With which that name is not entwined.

That name lights up the thickest gloom,
    All my base fears its sweetness shames.
Let nothing then displease my soul,
    In which I read that name of names.

Let God come near, and all is well;
    His presence cheers my roughest road;
And nothing shall depress my heart,
    In which I read the love of God.

Come life or death, come tears or smiles,
    Let me still trust and not despair;
I shrink not from the stormiest cloud,
    If but the joy of God be there.

UP THE HILL.

PRESS up the hill!
 The view its summit shows is fair and
  wide,—
Greenness of field and forest on each side:
Let the eye drink its fill.

Press up the hill!
 Others have climbed before thee this rough
  slope,
 And now are calmly resting on its top,
Where the soft dews distil.

Press up the hill!
 It is the mount, the holy mount of God;
 Dread not the steepness of the narrow road,
Nor the air sharp and chill.

Press up the hill!
 By it the radiant city-gate is won,
 And from its height we see the rising sun:
Then upward, upward still!

WATCHING FOR THE MASTER.

WATCH, for ye know not when the Master cometh,
  At midnight, or at cock-crow, or at morn;
When stars die out, and earth is all awaiting
  For the first streak which tells that day is born.

Long has He tarried, long His weary household
  Have, from their eastern lattice, looked and sighed.
Why comes He not? their eyes and hearts are failing,
  With faith and hope so long and sorely tried.

Through the cold ages, when abounding evil
  Chilled their warm love, they watched, but watched in vain.

The foe waxed stronger, faith and hope grew
　　weaker ;—
　'Lord, come,' they cried, again and yet again.

Again and yet again; but still He came not:
　Dark centuries of evil came and went.
'O Master, tarry not,' they cried.　He spake
　not.
　It seemed an everlasting banishment.

Evil still reigned ; the good still few and feeble,
　The church's haters numerous and strong ;
Error more subtle, truth more sad and silent,
　Faith's anguished cry still rising, Lord, how
　　long !

Long has the world, the Master's rule dis-
　owning,
　Hating His presence and His holy sway,
Cried, 'Where is now the promise of his com-
　ing,
　And where the signs of the long-promised
　　day ?'

But still, above the scoff, and taunt, and laughter,
　The still small voice ariseth, 'Watch and pray;'
And still, to cheer the hours of lonely waiting,
　'Behold, I come,' we hear the Master say.

It may be that the night will yet grow darker,
　It may be that the storm is not yet spent;
It may be that the times will wax more evil,
　Earth braving heaven, and scorning to repent.

It may be that the church's eye shall weary,
　That hope, so long deferred, at last shall faint;
That dark delay the buoyant heart may sadden,
　And shake the faith of many an eager saint.

Still let us hear the Master daily saying,
　Behold, I come; awake, arise, prepare!
For but a little, and there sounds the summons,
　Ascend, my saints, to meet me in the air!

Then end at once our weary years of watching:
    Cometh the vision and the vernal day;
Cometh the Master to His waiting household;
    The sunlight bursts, the shadows flee away!

Error and darkness hide their heads for ever,—
    Truth, light, and righteousness make up our morn;
Earth rises up in newer, holier splendour,
    Than when at first in perfect beauty born.

IN HIM WAS LIFE.

FAIR world of earth, and air, and clouds, and sea,
   Full of sweet wisdom and rich goodness thou!
   Yet all the glories beaming on thy brow
Are not thine own, though seen so bright in thee.

Life leaps, and laughs, and sings aloud in glee,
   In man, and beast, and bird, and tree, and flower;
   Yet each of these doth cry out hour by hour,
'I am not Life; THE Life is not in me.'

And beauty shineth, smileth everywhere,
   In heavens above, and on this earth beneath;
   Yet with clear voice each bright thing brightly saith,
'I am not Beauty; I am only fair.'

Joy, too, all nature has with splendour clad;
  The sounds that fill the music-haunted air,
  Or rise from forest or from stream, declare,
'I am not gladness; I am only glad.'

O wondrous sun! with all that light of thine,
  Unchanged since thy Creator kindled thee,
  The fountainhead of radiant purity;
Thou say'st, 'I am not light, I only shine.'

Look not to me, say earth, and sea, and sky,
  We but reveal another's comeliness;
  As voices crying in the wilderness,
'The birth-place of all beauty is on high.'

THE DOUBLE STAR.

L ONG ages came and went;
And, sick with hope deferred,
The church's voice grew faint; she seemed
Unnoticed and unheard.
At length to her a child was born,
At length a son was given;
The dayspring broke on earth,
The love came down from heaven.

Long years have come and gone,
And with uplifted eye,
The church, with calm and silent hope,
Has watched the eastern sky.
At length the voice shall yet be heard,
With which all earth shall ring:
Lo, this is God, our God,
This the long-promised King.

THE LIGHT OF THE RISEN ONE.

RISEN Son of God, this day
    Pour on us Thy rising ray!
All our light, O Risen One,
Cometh from Thy light alone.

Let Thy cross upon us shine,
With its love and power divine;
    Beams of everlasting grace
    Flowing to us from Thy face.

From Thy grave let light come forth,
Breaking o'er a darkened earth;
    Resurrection-light and peace,
    Resurrection-joy and bliss.

In Thy life alone is light,
And without it all is night;
    From the darkness of the tomb,
    Light of life, arise and come.

ENTER INTO THY CLOSET.

SHUT in with God, as in His tent,
    No veil of earth let down between;
We look beyond that firmament,
    And enter on a world unseen.

We would behold Him face to face,
    And talk with Him, as friend with friend;
His fellowship of heavenly grace
    Enjoying without break or end.

As the disciples saw the Lord,
    And listened to His voice of love,
Still drinking in each heavenly word,
    Like living water from above;

So would we see Him, hear Him now,
    As if He spoke to us alone;
And so, shut out from all below,
    Would feast upon each look and tone.

UNBEGINNING AND UNENDING.

>Heri nostrum ; cras et pridem
>Semper tibi nunc et idem,
>Tuum, Deus, hodiernum,
>Indivisum sempiternum.—HILDEBERT.

UNBEGINNING and unending,
    Yet the Beginning and the Ending,
Thee, Jehovah, God of blessing,
Mighty God, Thy name confessing,
Mighty God, Thy greatness praising,
Hearts and voices upward raising,
Over us in mercy bending,
Ever down upon us sending
Daily fulness of all blessing,
Without measure, without ceasing,—
Thee Jehovah, great Creator,
Thee Jehovah, God of nature,
Thee the great and gracious Giver,
Thee we celebrate for ever,
Thee the first and last we sing,
Thee the high eternal King!

SABBATHS.

> Aurora cœlum purpurat
> Æther resultat laudibus,
> Mundus triumphans jubilat,
> Horrens avernus infremit.—OLD HYMN.

BRIGHT days, we need you in a world like this!
  Be brighter still,—ye cannot be too bright;
The world's six days of vanity and toil
  Would, but for you, oppress us with their night.

Bright days, in you heaven cometh nearer earth,
  And earth more fully breathes the balm of heaven:
The stillness of your air infuses calm,
  Fairest and sweetest of the weekly seven!

Your dews are fresher; greener spread your fields;
  Your streams flow by us with a sweeter song;

Your flowers give out a fragrance doubly soft,
  And the unwearied hours the joy prolong.

Ye are like openings in a cloudy sky,
    Through which we see the hidden blue
      beyond ;
Ye are like palm-trees in a wilderness,
    Where all is barrenness and death around.

Bright days, abide with us, we need you still !
    Ye are the ever-gushing wells of time ;
Ye are the open casements, where we hear
    The distant notes of heaven's descending
      chime.

HEAVENLY SUNSHINE.

> O sol salutis, intimis
> Jesu refulge mentibus,
> Dum, nocte pulsa, gratior
> Orbi dies renascitur.—OLD HYMN.

SUNSHINE of God, in thee my soul
    Would find her summer day:
O sunshine of the love of God,
    Thou leadest none astray.
Clear sunshine of the Book of God,
    Light up my shaded way;
Bright sunshine of the cross of Christ,
    For ever with me stay.
Fair sunshine of eternal life,
    Shed down on me thy ray;
All mist and shadow dissipate,
    All gloomy fears allay.
Within this clouded soul of mine
    Rule thou with blessed sway;
Thy radiant sweetness o'er each path
    Of shaded life display.

NEW-YEAR'S HYMN.

FROM THE LATIN.

Lapsus est annus ; redit annus alter ;
Vita sic mutis fugit acta pennis.

ONE year is gone ; another comes instead ;
    Thus our spent life on silent pinions
        flies ;
Thou, O our God, dost regulate their course,
    One Ruler of time's awful destinies.

Our nation, loaded with Thy gifts, gives
    praise ;
To Thee with one accord our country prays
That Thou for us wouldst still unchanged preserve
    The solemn faith and worship of old days.

Our citizens look up to Thee for food,
    And plead with Thee, that from their native
        shore

NEW-YEAR'S HYMN. 235

All sickness Thou wouldst drive away, and give
    Large blessings of sure peace for evermore.

They ask Thee graciously to pardon sin,
    Restoring what their guilt had reft away;
And, after grievous war, with Thy right hand
    To give the healthful palm of victory.

Hating the sins and stains of this vile life,
    Our hearts, O God, we consecrate to Thee:
Give happy years; and Thy paternal light
    Upon us resting may we ever see.

Whilst days run on, and rolling years return,
    And in fixed course the ages Thee obey,—
To Thee, the Three-one God, earth's Sovereign
    Lord,
    Let the wide world in song the homage pay.

SURGITE.

Do not slumber; suns are shining,—
  Shall they shine o'er thee in vain?
Be no sluggard; suns are setting
  Which shall never rise again.

All awake floats yonder eagle,
  In the bosom of the day,
Moving on through cloud and sunshine,
  Ever watching for his prey.

All awake stands yonder mountain,
  Its old eye all slumber shuns;
See its beacon-peaks still glowing
  With the gleam of ancient suns.

Never sleeping, never resting,
  On and on the rivers flow;
Every drop alive, and conscious
  Of a mighty work to do.

Do not dream away thy lifetime;
   'Twas not given thee for a dream:
'Tis a fragment of th' eternal,
   Which thou must, thou must redeem.

Every hour is more than golden,
   Every moment is a gem:
Treasure up these hours and moments,
   There are princely pearls in them.

Do not wanton with the wanton,
   Do not drivel with the fool;
Walk in truth with true men only,
   With the wise in wisdom's school.

Do not laugh away the immortal,
   Do not sport away the true;
Keep the noble and the manly
   Ever gloriously in view.

Be the coward in all evil,
   Flee its darkly-rolling wave;
In all good be ever foremost,
   Be the bravest of the brave.

Ever fervent, yet not fiery,
    From warm words thy lips restrain;
In the softness of the answer
    Thou wilt find thy power with men.

Speak thou calmly; men will listen
    To the calm of quiet souls:
Think thou firmly; men grow silent
    As the weighty thought unrolls.

Be no niggard of thy silver,
    Scatter freely, give in love;
Be large-hearted, open-handed,
    And the harvest thou shalt prove.

There was One who once gave freely,
    For His boundless all He gave;
And in giving He hath taught us
    How to give, and love, and save.

And Himself the Truth, the True One,
    He came the truth to show,
That the treasure, without measure,
    All His wisdom we might know.

SURGITE.

Truth has many sides, consider,—
    Keep its many sides in view;
Mark each face of its clear crystal,
    Go round and round the true.

Do not loiter; time is rushing,
    Like the racer to the goal:
Do not waste the eternal treasure,
    Do not fling away thy soul.

Do not linger; see the ages
    Are rushing to their doom,
And the long eternal era
    Is coming in their room.

Do not trifle; earth is groaning
    Under wrongs and burdens sore:
Be in earnest; put thy shoulder
    To the work that lies before.

Be no lounger; do not fritter
    All thy little life away:
See, its hours are all in motion,
    And they will not for thee stay.

Live for spirit, not for matter;
    Aim thou higher every hour:
Leave the steaming swamps beneath thee,
    Be thy home the mountain-tower.

Look thou far into the future,
    Far beyond that sky and sea;
Seek to show thyself here daily
    What thou hopest soon to be.

Be not selfish; earth's great sickness
    Needeth self-denying men
To go forth among the dying,
    And to soothe the beds of pain.

Doff the purple, don the armour,
    Take the helmet and the shield;
Drop the garland, seize the weapon,
    Make thee haste to take the field.

Lie not down among the roses,
    Carry high thy cross and sword;
What! A Sybarite disciple
    Of a self-denying Lord!

Be not weary; for the warfare,
  Hard and fierce, will soon be o'er;
And the rest will be unchanging
  On the green unfading shore.

Fear no foemen, be their number
  Like the locusts in their flight;
He who leads thee is the Captain
  Who has never lost a fight.

Name His name, and speed thee onward:
  'Tis a spell of strength, that name;
'Tis a battle-cry resistless,
  Striking foes with dread and shame.

Be not idle; kings are girding
  Their last sword upon their thigh;
And the long-expected battle
  Of the world is drawing nigh.

Be not heedless; mark the lightning
  That is treasured in yon cloud:
See the store of silent thunder
  That so soon shall speak aloud.

Up! be watching; Christ is coming,—
   He is coming for His own;
He is coming to do battle
   For His long expected crown.

When the evil is most evil,
   When the foe is in his strength,
And earth's fever universal,
   Then the Healer comes at length.

And when fails all human wisdom,
   When man's boasted light succumbs,
When his progress proves illusion,
   Then the world's one Prophet comes.

When the last, wide, lawless uproar
   Showeth man's poor rule all vain;
Then the mighty King descendeth
   In His glorious power to reign.

When man's wisdom turns to folly,
   And his faith is but a name;
When his self-will, vainly seeking
   High dominion, ends in shame.

When his art, and thought, and culture
  Do but swell the turbid stream;
When his reason struggles vainly,
  And the mind-power proves a dream.

When the tree of knowledge ripens
  Its bitterest and its last;
When the era of believing
  Into unbelief has past.

When the learning of the ages
  Cannot cleanse the world's foul air;
When the spirits of the faithful
  Are slow sinking in despair.

Then the wisdom of all wisdoms
  Poureth in upon our night;
And the many masters vanish,
  The One Teacher comes in light..

Up! be watching; stars are paling,.
  Day is breaking o'er the deep,
And the tempest of the ages
  Is subsiding into sleep.

When the shadow rests most sadly
　　Over earth, and all is fear,
Lift we up our head in triumph,—
　　Our redemption draweth near.

When the warfare rages fiercest,
　　Then His hosts our Captain cheers;
When the darkness is the darkest,
　　Then the morning star appears.

PSALMS.

PSALM XXXVII. L. M.

FRET not at sinners! Envy not
    The workers of iniquity!
As grass they quickly are cut down,
    As the green herb they fade away.

Trust in Jehovah, and do good;
    Dwell in the land, and feed secure:[1]
Yea, in the Lord delight thyself,
    He will thy heart's desires make sure.

Upon Jehovah roll thy way;
    Trust Him, and He will do it all.
As light thy righteousness, as noon
    Thy judgment, yet bring forth He shall.

Rest in Jehovah: for Him wait!
    Fret not thyself at his success
Who prospereth in his evil way,
    And brings to pass his wickedness.

[1] See Hebrew.

Be still from anger; wrath forsake:
    Fret not thyself; 'tis evil all.[1]
Slain are the sinners; they on God
    Who wait, the earth inherit shall.

For yet a little while, and then
    The wicked one no more is seen;
His place thou ponderest, and lo!
    It is as it had never been.

And then, for their inheritance,
    The meek ones shall the earth possess;
Yea, then they shall delight themselves
    In the abundance of Thy peace.

Gnashing his teeth, the wicked one
    Against the just one plots doth lay;
The Lord shall laugh at him, because
    He sees at hand his coming day.

The wicked have unsheathed the sword;
    Yea, they have bent their bow to slay
The poor and needy one,—to smite
    All those who are of upright way.

---

[1] See Hebrew.

Their sword shall enter their own heart;
    Their bows be shivered! Better far
The just one's little all, than stores
    Of the ungodly many are.

Broken shall be the wicked's arms;
    Jehovah still the just sustains.
Jehovah knows the upright's days,
    Their heritage for aye remains.

They, when the time of evil comes,
    Shall never disappointed be;
Yea, in the days of dearth they shall
    Be satisfied abundantly.

For perish shall the wicked ones,
    And, as the fat of lambs, shall be
Jehovah's foes: they shall consume,—
    In smoke they shall consume away.

The wicked borrows, none he pays;
    The just is kind and liberal.
They whom God blesseth take the earth,
    They whom He curseth perish all.

Man's[1] steps are ordered by the Lord,
   And he delighteth in His way.
He falleth, yet is not o'erthrown :
   Jehovah's hand doth him upstay.

I have been young, and now am old,
   And yet the just one never did
I see forsaken of the Lord,
   Nor yet his offspring begging bread.

Loving is he always, and lends;
   For his seed blessing is in store.
Depart from evil, and do good,
   Thou shalt abide for evermore.

For judgment doth Jehovah love,
   And He will not forsake His own.
For evermore are they preserved ;
   The sinner's offspring is o'erthrown.

The righteous shall inherit earth,
   And on it they shall dwell for aye ;
The righteous wisdom uttereth,
   His tongue doth judgment speak alway.

[1] See Hebrew.

The law of God is in his heart,
  None of his steps shall slide away;
The wicked for the righteous one
  Watcheth, and seeketh him to slay.

Surely Jehovah will not leave
  The just one in the wicked's hand;
Nor against him will sentence give
  When he shall in the judgment stand.

Upon Jehovah wait, and keep
  His way; so He exalt shall thee
Earth to inherit: when the fall
  Of the ungodly thou shalt see.

I've seen the wicked one in power,
  Outspreading like a green bay-tree:
He passeth, and lo! he is not;
  I sought, but found he could not be.

Watch thou the perfect one, and see
  The upright, for his end is peace;
But the transgressors perish all,
  The sinner's end destruction is.

But from Jehovah ever is
    Salvation to the righteous all;
And in each season of distress,
    Their succour prove Jehovah shall.

Jehovah hath them helped and saved,
    And He will yet deliver them;
Yea, save them from the wicked hands,
    Because they trusted in His name.

PSALM XXXVIII.   10's.

JEHOVAH, in Thy wrath rebuke me not,
   Nor in Thy hot displeasure me chastise;
For fast within me do Thine arrows stick,
   And upon me right sore Thy hand it lies.

There is no soundness in my flesh, because
   Of this Thy wrath; no peace[1] my bones
     within,
Because of these my great iniquities,
   For far above my head has passed my sin.

A burden much too heavy are my sins,
   With hateful wounds they cover all my
     frame;
I'm troubled, I am greatly bowèd down
   All the day long with mourning and with
     shame.

[1] See Hebrew.

PSALM XXXVIII.

Unclean, unclean am I from head to foot;
   No health in me; weak and all bruised I lie;
By reason of my heart's disquietude,
   I lifted have my loud and bitter cry.

All my desire I lay before Thee, Lord,
   Nor from Thee hidden is my secret groan;
Panteth my heart, quite faileth me my strength,
   The light of these mine eyes is from me gone.

Lovers and neighbours from my stroke stand off;
   My nearest stand the farthest: snares they lay,
My soul who seek; yea, they who seek my hurt
   Speak mischief, and plot falsehoods all the day.

But as one deaf, so heard I not at all;
   My mouth I opened not, as one that's dumb:
Thus was I as a man that heareth not,
   One from whose mouth doth no reproving come.

For in Thee, O Jehovah, have I hoped;
  Yea, Thou, O Lord my God, wilt hear my
    cries.
For I have said, What if they should prevail?
  When my foot slips, against me they arise.

For I am ever halting, and my grief
  Has without ceasing still before me been:
For mine iniquity I will declare;
  Yea, I will bitterly bewail my sin.

For lively are my foes,—yea, they are strong;
  They that me falsely hate are multiplied.
They are my foes that render ill for good,
  Because I seek the good, and there abide.

But, O Jehovah, do not me forsake;
  And, O my God, be Thou not far from me.
Make haste, O Lord, to give me needed help,
  For my salvation is alone from Thee.

PSALM XXXIX.

I SAID, I will keep watch upon my ways,
    That so my tongue I may from sin restrain;
And while the wicked one before me stands,
    I to my mouth will hold the needful rein.

Dumb with my silence was I; yea, from good
    I held my peace; yet grief more fierce became:
My heart within me waxèd yet more hot,
    Till, as I mused, thus blazed the pent-up flame.

I spake thus with my tongue: Make me, O Lord,
    To know the end of this my life below,
And what the measure of my days on earth,
    That all my frailty I may fully know.

Behold, an handbreadth Thou hast made my
    days,
  Mine age as nothing is before Thine eye:
Ah, surely every man on earth that is,
  Even at his best estate, is vanity.

Ah, surely in a vain show walketh man,
  Surely they troubled are for vanity.
He heapeth up his treasures on the earth,
  And doth not know for whom they gathered
    be.

And now, what have I waited for, O Lord?
  My hope is resting only upon Thee.
Me from my manifold transgressions save;
  Of fools the scorn, oh make not, make not
    me.

Dumb was I, and my mouth I opened not,
  Because 'twas Thou, O Lord, who didst it
    all.
Lift off Thy blows; I am consumed by these
  Sharp battle-strokes which from Thy hand
    do fall.

With Thy rebukes for sin Thou chastenest
  man ;
  Even as the moth, to melt and pass away
Thou makest all his comely excellence :
  Ah, surely every man is vanity !

Hear, O Jehovah, hear at length my prayer ;
  Unto my supplicating cry Thine ear
Incline ; O Lord, no longer silence keep ;
  Oh, keep not silence at my falling tear.

For I a stranger am with Thee, O Lord ;
  A sojourner, as all my fathers were.
Oh spare me, that I may be comforted,
  Ere earth I leave, and am no longer there.

PSALM XL.

Waiting, I waited for the Lord;
    He stooped to me, and heard my cry;
From the dark pit and miry clay
    He brought me up and set on high.

My feet He lifted to the rock,
    Established hath He all my ways;
A new song in my mouth He put,—
    To God, our God, a song of praise.

Many shall see, and fear, and trust
    Upon the Lord. That man is blest,
Who, heeding not the proud and false,
    Doth in Jehovah find his rest.

Many and mighty are the works
    Which Thou, O Lord my God, hast wrought;
Thy purposes to us-ward, they
    Have wondrous been beyond all thought.

Who can them reckon up? Who can
  Set them in order Thee before?
Would I declare and speak of them?
  Than can be numbered they are more!

Not to the flesh of sacrifice
  Hast Thou, Jehovah, had regard:
Not in the offering hadst delight;—
  These ears of mine Thou hast prepared.

Not for the whole burnt-sacrifice,
  Not for sin-offering didst Thou look.
Then did I speak, Behold, I come!
  Of me 'tis written in the Book:

To do Thy pleasure, O my God,
  Has been the gladness of my heart;
Yea, and Thy law hath ever been
  Deep hidden in my inmost part.

The tidings of the righteousness
  In the assembly great I've shown:
My lips, behold, I kept not back;
  This, O Jehovah, Thou hast known.

Within the chambers of my heart
    Thy righteousness I did not hide;
But I have all Thy faithfulness
    And Thy salvation testified.

Within the great assembly I
    Thy love and truth left not untold;
Thy loving-kindnesses from me,
    Jehovah, do Thou not withhold.

Thy loving-kindness and Thy truth,
    Let them preserve me constantly;
For evils past all numbering
    On every side encompass me.

My sins of me have taken hold,
    So that mine eyes no longer see;
More than the hairs upon my head!
    Therefore my heart forsaketh me.[1]

Be pleased, Jehovah, me to save;
    To help, Jehovah, make no stay:
Who seek my soul to lay it waste,
    Confounded and ashamed be they.

[1] See Hebrew.

Turned back be they and put to shame,
    Who joy in mine adversity;
Laid waste be they for shaming me,
    Aha, aha, to me who cry.

Joyful and glad in Thee be all
    Whose hearts are set on Thee above;
Great be Jehovah, let them say,
    All they who Thy salvation love.

But I all poor and needy am;
    Yet me the Lord hath not forgot.
Help and deliverer art Thou;
    Make haste, my God, and tarry not!

PSALM XLI.

O BLESSED he who on the poor one thinks!
   In trouble's day Jehovah will him save.
Jehovah will him keep, yea, save alive;
   And in the land he blessedness shall have.

And not unto the will of enemies
   Wilt Thou at any time, Lord, give him o'er.
Jehovah on his sick-bed holds him up;
   His bed Thou smoothest all in sickness sore.

I said, Jehovah, unto me show grace!
   Heal me, for sin against Thee I have done.
My enemies against me evil speak;
   When shall he perish and his name be gone?

Yea, when he comes, it is to spy me out;
   And with his lips he speaketh vanity.
His heart doth gather mischief to itself;
   He goeth out, and publishes the lie.

All they who hate me whisper in their plots;
    Against me they devise an evil sore.
There cleaves to him, say they, some cursed
    thing;
    He lieth there, and shall arise no more.

Man of my peace, my friend, my trusted one,
    Guest of my table, he doth me betray:
But Thou, Jehovah, unto me show grace;
    Oh raise me up, that I may them repay.

By this I know Thou lovest me, because
    My foe, o'er me to triumph, finds no place.
And me, in mine uprightness, Thou hast kept,
    For ever setting me before Thy face.

Now blessed be Jehovah, Israel's God,
    Blest be Jehovah from eternity,
To the eternity that is to come!—
    Amen, Amen, Jehovah blessed be!

PSALM XLII.

AS pants for water-brooks the hart,
    So pants my soul, O God, for Thee;
For God it thirsts, the living God:
    When shall I go my God to see?

My tears have been my bitter meat,
    All the night long and all the day;
While unto me continually,
    Where is thy God? my haters say.

When I these days to mind recall,
    I pour out all my soul in me;
For once in other days had I
    Gone with the mighty company.

With them into the house of God
    I went, with voice of joy and praise:
With the great multitude I went
    That kept the solemn holidays.

Why art thou then cast down, my soul?
   And why disquieted in me?
Hope thou in God: I shall Him praise;
   His face shall my salvation be.

My God, my soul is bowed down,
   My soul is bowed down in me;
From Jordan, Hermon, Mizar hill,
   My God, I will remember Thee!

With thunder of Thy waterspouts,
   Deep, answering to deep, doth call;
Thy breakers break above my head,
   And o'er me roll Thy billows all.

Yet in the day Jehovah will
   Command for me His tender care:
His song is with me all the night;
   God of my life, oh hear my prayer.

I unto God my rock will say,
   Why hast Thou me forgotten so?
Why must I go still mourning on,
   Because of the oppressing foe?

As with a sword my bones within,
 My foes me with reproaches load;
While without ceasing, day by day,
 They say to me, Where is thy God?

Why art thou, O my soul, cast down?
 And why disquieted in me?
Hope thou in God; I shall Him praise:
 Health of my face, my God is He!

PSALM XLIII.

JUDGE me, O God, my God, and plead my
    cause
With an ungodly nation; from the man
Of fraud and wickedness deliver me,
    For of my strength Thou art the God alone.

Why dost Thou cast me off? Why go I thus
    Mourning because mine enemies oppress?
Send out Thy light and truth; me lead, me
    guide
    To Thine abode,—Thy hill of holiness.

Then to the altar of my God I'll come,
    To God the gladness of my joy I'll go:
Yea, with the harp I will give thanks to Thee;
    To Thee, O God, my God, my praise shall
    flow.

Why art thou thus dejected, O my soul?
   And why art thou disquieted in me?
Hope thou in God, for I shall yet Him praise;
   Health of my countenance, my God, is He.

---o---

PSALM XLIV.

WE with our ears have heard, O God,
   Our fathers have to us made known
The work which Thou in times of old,
   Even in their days, for them hast done.

For Thou the heathen hast cast out,
   Planting Thy chosen in their stead.
The nations Thou afflicted hast;
   Thine own to multiply hast made.

Not by their sword the land they got,
   Nor by their arm salvation came:
Thy hand it was, Thine arm, Thy face
   Of light; because Thou lovedst them.

Thou art my King, O God! Send help
  To Jacob! All our enemies
Through Thee we smite; and through Thy
    name
  We crush those that against us rise.

Not in my bow put I my trust,
  Not through this sword deliverance came;
'Tis Thou who from our foes hast saved,
  And all our haters put to shame.

In God, who hath done all for us,
  In God we glory all the day;
Unto Thy name, O Lord our God,
  We will give praise eternally.

But Thou hast cast us off, and shamed,
  No longer leading our array:
Back from the foe Thou mak'st us turn;
  Our haters take us for their prey.

As sheep for food Thou givest us,
  And scattered us on heathen ground;
Thy people Thou hast sold for nought,
  No profit by their price hast found.

PSALM XLIV.

As a reproach Thou hast us set,
    A scorn and jest on every side;
A byword among men are we,
    They see us only to deride.

Confusion is before my face,
    And shame hath wholly covered me
From him who slanders and blasphemes,
    From the avenging enemy.

All this has come on us, O Lord,
    Yet have we not forgotten Thee,
Nor from Thy covenant turned aside
    To falsehood and apostasy.

Our heart has not gone back; nor turned
    Our goings from Thy ways of light.
In savage haunts Thou smitedst us,
    And wrapt us in death's shade of night.

If we the name of God, our God,
    Forgotten have, or stretched our hands
To idols, shall not God this search?
    For He all secrets understands.

Truly for Thy name's sake, O Lord,
    All the day long to death we're driven;
And counted by our enemies
    A flock of sheep to slaughter given.

Arise! Why sleepest Thou, O Lord?
    Awake! for ever leave us not:
Oh wherefore hidest Thou Thy face?
    Hast Thou our grief and woe forgot?

Our soul is to the dust bowed down,
    Our body cleaveth to the ground:
Arise! give help, and us redeem,
    Because Thy mercies, Lord, abound.

PSALM XLVI.[1]

GOD is for us a refuge and a strength,
    A very present help in troublous days;
And therefore will we never be afraid,
    Even when the earth is shaken to its base.

Yea, when the mighty mountains shall be swept
    Into the depths of the devouring sea;
When vexed and troubled are its swelling streams,
    And mountains with its heavings shivered be.

River, whose streams God's city shall make glad!
    O holy dwelling of the Highest One;
God in the midst of her! she cannot move!
    Yea, God her help when the great morn shall dawn!

---

[1] For Psalm xlv., see 3d Series of *Hymns of Faith and Hope*.

The heathen raged, and moved the kingdoms
    were;
His voice He uttered, earth did melt away.
The Lord, the Lord of hosts is with us still,
    And Jacob's God our refuge and our stay.

Come, see Jehovah's works! What ruin He
    Brings on the earth! All wars throughout
        He stays;
He breaks the bow, the spear in sunder cuts,
    The chariot gives to the consuming blaze.

Be still, and know that I am God! Among
    The heathen will I sit in majesty;
Throughout the limits of the utmost earth
    Will I, Jehovah, be exalted high.

Jehovah, He Himself is on our side;
    The Lord of hosts abideth with us aye;
The mighty God of Jacob, He it is
    Who is alone our refuge and our stay.

PSALM XLVII.

OH clap your hands, ye nations all;
    Shout unto God with voice of mirth!
The Lord most High is terrible,
    Great King is He o'er all the earth.

He breaks the nations under us,
    The people all beneath our feet;
Our heritage for us He chose,
    Of Jacob whom He loved, the seat.

God with a shout ascends the throne,
    Jehovah with the trumpet's voice;
Sing psalms to God, sing psalms, sing psalms,
    Before our King with psalms rejoice.

For King of all the earth is God,
    A psalm of wisdom sing, oh sing;
God o'er the nations reigns, God sits
    Upon His holy throne as King.

Princes of nations gathered are,
  Of Abraham's God the tribes draw nigh.
To God belong the shields of earth,
  And greatly is He set on high.

———o———

PSALM XLVIII.

JEHOVAH, great is He!
  The mighty praise is His,
Within the city of our God,
  His hill of holiness.

O beautiful of place,
  The gladness of all lands,—
Thou Zion hill; ye slopes of north,—
  The great King's city stands!

God in her palaces
  Is known for rock and stay;
For, lo! the kings, against her met,
  Together passed away.

They saw, and as they gazed
    They marvelled at the sight;
Troubled and terror-smitten, they
    Betook themselves to flight.

Fear seized upon them there!
    Like travail-pangs their thrall;
And with Thy east wind Thou hast
    wrecked
    The ships of Tarshish all.

That which our ears have heard,
    Thou to our eyes hast showed,
Within Thy city, Lord of hosts,
    The city of our God.

God will establish her,
    For aye her bulwark prove;
And in Thy courts, O God, have we
    Made mention of Thy love.

As is Thy name, so is
    Thy praise through earth abroad;
And full of glorious righteousness
    Is Thy right hand, O God.

Let Zion hill rejoice,
　Let Judah's daughters praise,
Because of all Thy judgments, Lord,
　Thy true and righteous ways.

Compass ye Zion round!
　And number ye her forts;
Note well her bulwarks and her towers,
　Mark ye her royal courts.

That ye may tell it all
　To ages yet to come;
This God, our God for evermore,
　Will guide us o'er the tomb.

PSALM XLIX.

HEAR this, ye people all,
    Ye dwellers on earth's sphere.
Sons of the low, sons of the high,[1]
    Both rich and poor, give ear.

Of wisdom and of truth
    The words my mouth shall fill;
The musings of my heart shall be
    Of understanding still.

To parable and song
    Mine ear I will apply,
And on my harp will I unfold
    Thy words of mystery.

They trust in wealth, they boast
    Of riches; yet who can
With all their gold in any wise
    Redeem a brother man?

[1] See Hebrew.

(For ransom-price to God
    Their gold availeth not.
Too precious the redemption is,—
    Too costly to be bought.)

Which of all these the life
    Immortal can bestow,—
To save his fellow-man, that he
    Should no corruption know?

He sees the wise man die,
    And the fool pass away,
Forsaking all their substance here,
    For others to make way.

Houses and dwellings all
    From age to age the same
Shall be, they think in heart; their
        lands
By their own names they name.

Yet man in honour placed,
    Abideth not a day;
But like the cattle of the field,
    He passes hence away.

Such is their course on earth,
    Such is their foolish way;
Yet those who after them arise
    Delight in what they say.

On to the grave like sheep
    They pass, of death the prey;
The righteous in the coming morn
    Shall over them have sway.

Their beauty in the grave
    Shall lie, and there consume;
God from the grave redeems my soul,
    He plucks me from the tomb.

Then fear not when a man
    With riches great shall be,
Or when the glory of his house
    Increases mightily.

He dies, and nothing takes
    Of all he here shall have;
Nor shall his glory after him
    Descend into the grave.

In life he blest his soul,
  A happy man was he;
And so, when thou art prosperous,
  Men will speak well of thee.

Where all his fathers are,
  There shall he gathered be;
But never, never more shall they
  The light of morning see.

Man, though in honour placed,
  Refuses to be wise;
And thus, like cattle of the field,
  He perishes and dies.

INDEX OF FIRST LINES.

	PAGE
Acquaint thyself with God,	61
Age of the ages,	164
All night upon the city-wall,	85
Among the many, I am lost and weary,	42
As pants for water-brooks the hart,	265
Ascribe ye strength to God,	59
Bright days, we need you in a world like this,	231
Brothers, wherefore fear ye?	183
By sleep He consecrated sleep,	82
Come, all ye nations, utter all your praises,	58
Deep calleth unto deep,	147
Do not slumber: suns are shining,	236
Ere long we shall be full; as night by night,	84
Eternal Father, gracious One,	66
Fair world of earth, and air, and clouds, and sea,	225
Food of the soul, eternal bread,	129

	PAGE
For the bread and for the wine,	131
For the first time I see,	150
Fret not at sinners! Envy not,	247
Give thou thy youth to God,	117
Giver of rest,	140
God is for us a refuge and a strength,	273
Good is Thy will, O Lord, and good Thy way,	127
Good night, ye gems of beauty,	25
Great Lord and Master of the temple, come,	184
He died to live; for Jesus died,	107
He must increase, and I decrease,	209
Hear this, ye people all,	279
Hem of the seamless robe,	144
Holy Spirit, spring of gladness,	157
I am crucified with Christ,	189
I lay up treasure in the heavens,	52
I said, I will keep watch upon my ways,	256
I suffer, that I may behold, when pain,	40
I was in love with hill and vale,	102
In God, your God, be strong,	199
In the death of Christ I die,	174
In this great world of ours,	216
In vain, in vain with human love,	111
Is good or evil reigning here,	192
It draweth near,	1
Jehovah, great is He,	276
Jehovah, in Thy wrath rebuke me not,	253
Judge me, O God, my God, and plead my cause,	268

INDEX.

	PAGE
Keep silence, God is speaking,	207
King of kings ! ascend Thy throne,	30
Lead us, O Lord, to Bethlehem,	93
Let me call nothing dark or ill,	219
Light of life, so softly shining,	113
Light of the world ! All the earth is waiting,	56
Long ages came and went,	227
My mother earth,	32
My past, O Lord, with all its scenes,	180
My tempted soul, arise and fight,	176
No distance now ! the far-off and the near,	78
Now at the Father's side,	104
O blessed he who on the poor one thinks,	263
O clap your hands, ye nations all,	275
O early saved,	155
O ye of little faith,	70
On both sides is my anchor firmly cast,	169
On his Lord's bosom now,	203
One year is gone ; another comes instead,	234
Only one cross,	148
Out in the dew and cold He stands,	172
Out of darkness into light,	99
Poor stranger, in the Master's name,	62
Praise ye the Lord, all things that be,	101
Press up the hill,	220

	PAGE
Quickly bright life withers,	90
Rejoice, my soul, the Christ has come,	181
Risen Son of God, this day,	228
Rock of the desert, pouring still,	48
Shut in with God, as in His tent,	229
Sing, ancient wind,	114
Sinks the swift sun; yet sinks but to arise,	51
Speak Thou to me, O Son of God,	122
Sunshine of God, in thee my soul,	233
Sure anchor of the soul,	76
Sure the record; Christ has come,	97
Take these things hence,	44
That which hath been is now,	74
The creeds have gone, so speaks the age,	194
The crowd sweeps onward still,	37
The farewell is complete; the grave,	109
The Master hath His word fulfilled,	187
The Master saith, 'My time is now at hand,'	137
The old is better than the new,	46
The Son of God descends,	125
The time is short,	214
They die, and die not; theirs is life in death,	95
Thinner and thinner grows the veil,	201
Three hours the land was wrapt in gloom,	67
Thy yoke! All other yokes are hard,	196
Till He come we own His name,	134
'Tis a dead world through which I walk,	170
To my beloved ones my steps are moving,	28

	PAGE
Unbeginning and unending,	230
Unstable age,	159
Up to the fair myrrh-mountain,	22
Upon the Rock I plant my foot,	178
Waiting, I waited for the Lord,	259
Watch, for ye know not when the Master cometh,	221
We glory only in the cross,	69
We with our ears have heard, O God,	269
We yield to death: the fight is lost,	64
What! Know ye not,	211
When it is well with thee before thy God,	105
Ye know not what ye ask,	72

MURRAY AND GIBB, EDINBURGH,
PRINTERS TO HER MAJESTY'S STATIONERY OFFICE.

November, 1871.

A SELECTION FROM
JAMES NISBET AND CO.'S
LIST OF PUBLICATIONS.

LIGHT AND TRUTH. Bible Thoughts and Themes. Fifth and concluding volume. The Revelation of St. John. By the Rev. Horatius Bonar, D.D. Crown 8vo, 5s. cloth.

THE IRON HORSE; or, Life on the Line. A Railway Tale. By R. M. Ballantyne, author of "The Lifeboat," &c. With Illustrations. Crown 8vo, 5s. cloth.

ST. PAUL IN ROME; or, the Teachings, Fellowships, and Dying Testimony of the great Apostle in the City of the Cæsars. By the Rev. J. R. Macduff, D.D. With Vignette. Small crown 8vo, 4s. 6d. cloth.

A FOURTH EDITION OF THE EXPLANATORY AND PRACTICAL COMMENTARY ON THE NEW TESTAMENT; intended chiefly as a Help to Family Devotion. Edited and continued by the Rev. W. Dalton, B.D. Two volumes, 8vo, 24s. cloth.

INCIDENTS IN THE LIFE AND MINISTRY OF THE REV. A. R. C. DALLAS, M.A., Rector of Wonston. By His Widow. With Portrait. 8vo, 10s. 6d. cloth.

STORIES OF VINEGAR HILL. Illustrative of the Parable of the Sower. By the author of "The Golden Ladder." With coloured Illustrations. Small crown 8vo, 3s. 6d. cloth.

THE HOUSE IN TOWN. A sequel to "Opportunities." By the author of "The Wide Wide World," &c. With coloured Illustrations. Small crown 8vo, 2s. 6d. cloth.

THE ENJOYMENT OF LIFE; or, Religion in Relation to Pleasure. By the author of "The Mirage of Life." Crown 8vo, cloth.

SYNOPTICAL LECTURES ON THE BOOKS OF HOLY SCRIPTURE. First Series—Genesis to Canticles. By the Rev. Donald Fraser, M.A. Post 8vo, 6s. cloth.
"Singularly interesting, instructive, and comprehensive lectures."—*Record.*

WORKS PUBLISHED BY

MEMORY'S PICTURES. Poems by the author of "Memorials of Capt. Hedley Vicars," &c. Foolscap 8vo, 2s. 6d. cloth, gilt edges.

"A most elegant and attractive volume of poetry."—*Scattered Nation.*

DRAYTON HALL. Stories Illustrative of the Beatitudes. By the author of "Nettie's Mission," &c. With coloured Illustrations. Small crown 8vo, 3s. 6d. cloth.

"A pleasant book for boys."—*Literary World.*

WITHOUT AND WITHIN. A New England Story. With coloured Illustrations. Small crown 8vo, 3s. 6d cloth.

"The story is well told: the characters are well delineated; the pathetic and the humorous are skilfully blended."—*Maryland Church Record.*

JOHN OF THE GOLDEN MOUTH. A Life of Chrysostom, Preacher of Antioch, and Primate of Constantinople. By the Rev. W. MacGilvray, D.D. Post 8vo, 6s. cloth.

"A full, fresh, instructive, and interesting narrative."—*Weekly Review.*

THE DAY OF BEREAVEMENT; Its Lessons and its Consolations. By G. W. Mylne, Author of "Reposing in Jesus," &c. 16mo, 1s. 6d. cloth.

"Words *from* the heart, which will reach *to* the heart."—*Our Own Fireside.*

THE TIMES OF THE GENTILES; Being the 2520 Years from the First Year of Nebuchadnezzar (B.C. 623) to the 1260th Year of the Mohammedan Treading Down of Jerusalem, A.D. 1896. By the Rev. J. Baylee, D.D. Post 8vo, 5s. cloth.

"This book is fresh, and full of acute remark and pointed criticism on Scripture."—*Journal of Prophecy.*

EPISTOLA CONSOLATORIA. By Juan Perez, one of the Spanish Reformers in the Sixteenth Century. With a Life of the Author, by the late B. W. Wiffen. Small crown 8vo, 3s. 6d. cloth.

"There is more of God's word in the book than the author's; and its child-like devotional spirit will commend it always to the sorrowful."—*British and Foreign Evangelical Review.*

AN ENQUIRY INTO THE CHRISTIAN LAW AS TO THE RELATIONSHIPS WHICH BAR MARRIAGE. By the late Professor W. Lindsay, D.D. Small Crown 8vo, 2s. 6d. cloth.

"Dr. Lindsay is an able, acute, and logical reasoner."—*Record.*
"Model of controversial discussion."—*Presbyterian.*

HYMNS AND SONGS OF PILGRIM LIFE; or, Steps to the Throne. By the Rev. J. Gabb, B.A., Bulmer. Small crown 8vo, 2s. 6d. cloth.

"Worth reading—more than can be said of much modern poetry."—*Scattered Nation.*
"A collection of hymns and songs, many of them very sweet."—*Weekly Review.*

THE KING'S TABLE. The Lord's Supper in Letters to a Young Friend. By the Rev. G. PHILLIP, M.A., Edinburgh. 16mo, 8d. sewed, 1s. cloth.

"We do not aver that the little treatise before us has reached perfection, but it comes nearer the mark than anything we have lately met with."—*British and Foreign Evangelical Review.*

MEMORIES OF PATMOS; or, Some of the Great Words and Visions of the Apocalypse. By the Rev. J. R. MACDUFF, D.D. With Vignette. Post 8vo, 6s. 6d., cloth.

"Dr. Macduff has given us a volume of beautiful thoughts, and has clothed these thoughts with language which is at once elegant and forcible."—*Rock.*

MOSES THE MAN OF GOD. A Series of Lectures by the late JAMES HAMILTON, D.D., F.L.S. Small Crown 8vo, 5s., cloth.

"Graceful description, imaginative reconstruction, unconventional, and often very ingenious, sometimes learned disquisition, with the light graceful touch of poetic style and delicate fancy."—*British Quarterly Review.*

LAYS OF THE HOLY LAND. Selected from Ancient and Modern Poets by the Rev. HORATIUS BONAR, D.D. New Edition, with Illustrations from original Photographs and Drawings. Crown 4to, 12s., cloth.

"The Holy Land is a subject to which all great poets have devoted some of their best endeavours, and these are now brought together and adorned by illustrations worthy of such a text. . . . The volume will long remain a favourite."—*Times.*

THE FLOATING LIGHT OF THE GOODWIN SANDS. A Tale by R. M. BALLANTYNE, Author of "The Lifeboat," &c. With Illustrations. Crown 8vo, 5s. cloth.

"As full of incident, as healthy in tone, and as fresh and vigorous in style as any of its predecessors."—*Scotsman.*

A MISSIONARY OF THE APOSTOLIC SCHOOL. Being the Life of Dr. Judson, of Burmah. Revised and Edited by the Rev. HORATIUS BONAR, D.D. Small Crown 8vo, 3s. 6d., cloth.

"Very well written."—*Daily Review.* "Every way readable."—*Nonconformist.*

LITTLE ELSIE'S SUMMER AT MALVERN. By the Hon. Mrs. CLIFFORD BUTLER. Royal 16mo, 2s.6d. cloth. With Illustrations.

"A pleasing little story."—*Daily Telegraph.*

TOILING IN ROWING; or, Half-hours of Earnest Converse with my Hard-working Friends. By one who knows and loves them. Small Crown 8vo, 2s., cloth limp.

"An earnest, affectionate, and practical little book."—*Daily Review.*

A HISTORY OF THE REFORMATION FOR CHILDREN. By the Rev. E. NANGLE, B.A. With Illustrations. Three Volumes, 16mo, 4s. 6d. cloth.

WORKS PUBLISHED BY

PLEASANT FRUITS FROM THE COTTAGE AND THE CLASS. By Maria V. G. Havergal. Small Crown 8vo, 2s. 6d. cloth limp, 3s. cloth boards.

"Will be read with profit and delight."—*Our Own Fireside.*
"Peculiarly well suited for reading at District and Mothers' Meetings, &c."—*Church of England S. S. Magazine.*

WHAT SHE COULD, AND OPPORTUNITIES TO DO IT. By the Author of "The Wide Wide World." With Coloured Illustrations. Small Crown 8vo, 3s. 6d. cloth.

"A capital book for girls."—*Daily Review.*
"Clever and interesting little book."—*Glasgow Herald.*

FAITHFUL UNTO DEATH; or, Susine and Claude of the Val Pelice. By Anna Carolina di Tergolina. With Coloured Illustrations. Fcap. 8vo, 2s. 6d. cloth.

"Full of a pathos which will entrance the youthful reader."—*Weekly Review.*

GLEN LUNA; or, Dollars and Cents. By Anna Warner, Author of "The Golden Ladder." New Edition. With Coloured Illustrations. Small Crown 8vo, 3s. 6d. cloth.

"A really good tale."—*Rock.*
"Sure to increase in popularity."—*English Presbyterian Messenger.*

LOVE FULFILLING THE LAW. Stories on the Commandments. 16mo, 2s. 6d. cloth.

"Pretty and handy little book."—*Glasgow Herald.*

A PRACTICAL COMMENTARY ON THE GOSPEL ACCORDING TO ST. JOHN. In simple and familiar language. By G. B. Small Crown 8vo, 3s. 6d. cloth.

"We cordially recommend them as truly simple, earnest, and faithful comments."—*Our Own Fireside.*

NOTES OF OPEN-AIR SERMONS. By the Rev. Edward Walker, D.C.L., Rector of Cheltenham. Edited by a Member of the Congregation. Small Crown 8vo, 1s. 6d., cloth limp.

"Models of sound, faithful, and affectionate gospel preaching."—*English Presbyterian Messenger.*

THE ATONEMENT; in its Relations to the Covenant, the Priesthood, and the Intercession of our Lord. By the Rev. Hugh Martin, M.A. Post 8vo, 6s. cloth.

"A volume written with remarkable vigour and earnestness."—*British Quarterly Review.*
"Well worthy of a careful perusal, and we cordially recommend it to all our readers, and especially to ministers and students of theology."—*Evangelical Witness.*

THE SCRIPTURAL ACCOUNT OF CREATION VINDICATED BY THE TEACHING OF SCIENCE; or, A New Method of Reconciling the Mosaic and Geological Records of Creation. By the Rev. Wm. Paul, D.D. Post 8vo, 5s. cloth.

"Dr. Paul is entitled to the highest commendation for the extent and accuracy of his knowledge, and for the able, modest, and candid manner in which he applies it to his argument."—*Presbyterian.*

JAMES NISBET AND CO.

THE LIFE OF THE LATE JAMES HAMILTON, D.D., F.L.S. By the Rev. WILLIAM ARNOT, Edinburgh. Post 8vo, 7s. 6d. cloth. With Portrait.
"We rejoice to recommend this volume as a congenial and worthy record of one of the noblest and most fruitful lives with which the Church of Christ has been blessed in modern days. The editor's work has been done with admirable judgment."—*Weekly Review.*

A MEMOIR OF THE LATE REV. WILLIAM C. BURNS, M.A., Missionary to China. By Professor ISLAY BURNS, D.D., Glasgow. Crown 8vo, 6s. cloth. With Portrait.
"A more apostolic life has rarely been spent. . . . It is impossible to estimate too highly the good that may flow from this record of Christian life and labour."—*Sunday Magazine.*

THE LORD'S PRAYER. Lectures by the Rev. ADOLPH SAPHIR, B.A., Greenwich. Small Crown 8vo, 5s. cloth.
"A work so wide in its range of thought, and so concentrated in its doctrinal teachings, so rich and well packed, yet so simple and interesting, and so clear, pure, and intelligible in expression does not often make its appearance."—*Christian Work.*

CHRIST IN THE WORD. By the Rev. FREDERICK WHITFIELD, M.A., Author of "Voices from the Valley," &c. Small Crown 8vo, 3s. 6d. cloth.
"Very able and searching applications of spiritual truth."—*Our Own Fireside.*
"Excellent reading for the closet and family circle."—*Watchman.*

THE SHEPHERD AND HIS FLOCK; or, The Keeper of Israel and the Sheep of His Pasture. By the Rev. J. R. MACDUFF, D.D. With Vignette. Small Crown 8vo, 3s. 6d. cloth.
"A remarkably well-written volume, eminently practical and devout in its tone, and one which spiritually-minded persons will read with both pleasure and profit."—*Journal of Sacred Literature.*

ERLING THE BOLD. A Tale of the Norse Sea-Kings. By R. M. BALLANTYNE, Author of "The Lifeboat," &c. With Illustrations by the Author. Crown 8vo, 5s. cloth.
"The story is cleverly designed, and abounds with elements of romantic interest; and the author's illustrations are scarcely less vigorous than his text."—*Athenæum.*

LIGHT AND TRUTH. Bible Thoughts and Themes—First, Second, Third, and Fourth Series — 1. THE OLD TESTAMENT. 2. THE GOSPELS. 3. THE ACTS AND THE LARGER EPISTLES. 4. THE LESSER EPISTLES. 5. THE REVELATION OF ST. JOHN. By the Rev. HORATIUS BONAR, D.D. Crown 8vo, each 5s. cloth.
"Rich in matter and very suggestive."—*Christian Advocate.*
"Valuable work. It contains a series of brief expositions well suited for private use, or for family reading."—*Record.*

LECTURES ON HOSEA XIV. Preached in Portman Chapel during Lent, 1869. By the Rev. J. W. REEVE, M.A. Small Crown 8vo, 3s. 6d. cloth.
"It would be hard to over-estimate the amount of Gospel truth, practical exhortation, plain speaking, and affectionate interest in the spiritual welfare of his people, contained in these six lectures."—*Record.*

HE THAT OVERCOMETH; or, A Conquering Gospel. By the Rev. W. E. Boardman, M.A., Author of "The Higher Christian Life," &c. Small Crown 8vo, 3s. 6d. cloth.

"It is an excellent book for reading out on the Sabbath evenings in the family circle."—*Christian Work.*

THE SPANISH BARBER. A Tale, by the Author of "Mary Powell." Small Crown 8vo, 3s. 6d. cloth.

"A charming story for young and old, and most charmingly told."—*Rock.*
"An instructive story of missionary work in Spain."—*Christian Advocate.*

SERMONS. Preached at King's Lynn. By the late Rev. E. L. Hull, B.A. First and Second Series. Post 8vo, each 6s. cloth.

"This new volume of twenty sermons has all the claims of the first—the same happy use of Scripture, the same clear and firm grasp of the principle of every text he selected, the same earnest longing after the beauty and holiness on which he has now entered, the same play of imagination, the same freshness of thought, and fitness of utterance."—*Freeman.*

THE TITLES OF OUR LORD; A Series of Sketches for Every Sunday in the Christian Year, to be used in Bible-Class, Sunday School, and Private Study. By the Rev. Rowley Hill, M.A., Vicar of Frant. 16mo, 1s. 6d. cloth.

"The idea is excellent. . . . The matter is well arranged, free from repetitions, and in exposition thoroughly scriptural."—*Record.*

HEADS AND TALES; Or, Anecdotes and Stories of Quadrupeds and other Beasts. Compiled by Adam White, Duddingston. Second Edition. With Illustrations. Small Crown 8vo, 3s. 6d. cloth.

"Full of pleasant anecdotes."—*Times.*
"Amusing, instructive, and interesting."—*Standard.*

STEPPING HEAVENWARD. By Mrs. Prentiss. Author of "Little Susy's Six Birthdays," &c. With Coloured Illustrations. Small Crown 8vo, 2s. 6d. cloth.

"A faithful diary, recording the experiences of a good and gentle soul in its onward march to a better land."—*Rock.*

THE ROMANCE OF NATURAL HISTORY. First and Second Series. By P. H. Gosse, F.R.S. With many Illustrations. Post 8vo, each 7s. 6d. cloth; cheap edition, Small Crown 8vo, each 3s. 6d. cloth.

"A very pleasing and attractive work."—*Times.*
"It would be difficult to find more attractive gift books for the young."—*Record.*

BOOKS FOR WAYFARERS. By Anna Warner, Author of the "Golden Ladder." 32mo, cloth. 1. Wayfaring Hymns, Original and Selected. 6d. 2. The Melody of the Twenty-Third Psalm. 8d.

"There is an unction and a beauty about the books that well fit them to be pocket or table companions."—*Freeman.*
"Two little books, beautiful without and within."—*English Presbyterian Messenger.*

MEMORIALS OF THE LATE JAMES HEN-
DERSON, M.D., F.R.C.S.E. Medical Missionary to China. With Appendix. Small Crown 8vo, 3s. 6d. cloth. With Portrait. Also, Cheap and Abridged Edition, 16mo, 1s. cloth limp.

"The memorials of Dr. Henderson form as beautiful and exhilarating a little history as it has been for some time our task or pleasure to read. . . . . It is the story of one of those noble lives before which power and difficulty recoil, and give up the contest."—*Eclectic Review.*

MEMOIR AND REMAINS OF THE LATE REV.
JAMES D. BURNS, M.A., of Hampstead. By the late Rev. Dr. HAMILTON. With Portrait. Small Crown 8vo, 5s. cloth.

"It is not often that such sympathy of piety, friendship, and genius, exists between a biographer and his subject. It makes the book very precious—a memorial of the one as much as the other."—*British Quarterly Review.*

NOONTIDE AT SYCHAR; or, The Story of Jacob's
Well. By the Rev. J. R. MACDUFF, D.D. With Vignettes. Small Crown 8vo, 3s. 6d. cloth.

"One of the most attractive of the many pleasant and profitable religious studies published by Dr. Macduff."—*Daily Review.*

DEEP DOWN. A Tale of the Cornish Mines. By R. M.
BALLANTYNE, Author of "The Life Boat," etc. With Illustrations. Small Crown 8vo, 5s. cloth.

"This is just the subject for Mr. Ballantyne, whose stories in connection with that enterprise and adventure which have made England great are amongst the best of modern days."—*Daily News.*

FAMILY PRAYERS FOR FOUR WEEKS. With
Additional Prayers for Especial Days and Occasions. By the Very Rev. HENRY LAW, M.A., Dean of Gloucester. Small Crown 8vo, 3s. 6d. cloth.

"Thoroughly sound and scriptural, and really devotional."—*Christian Observer.*

LIFE OF THE LATE REV. JOHN MILNE, M.A., of
Perth. By the Rev. HORATIUS BONAR, D.D. With Portrait. Crown 8vo, 6s. cloth.

"Written with the elegance, sound judgment, and good feeling which were to be expected from Dr. Bonar; and being given to a large extent in the autobiographical form, it is, on that account, the more trustworthy and valuable."—*British and Foreign Evangelical Review.*

A COMMENTARY ON ST. PAUL'S EPISTLE TO
THE GALATIANS. With Sermons on the Principal Topics contained in it. By the Rev. EMILIUS BAYLEY, B.D., Vicar of St. John's, Paddington. Crown 8vo, 7s. 6d. cloth.

"Admirable commentary. It is full of well arranged and well digested matter, and without any pedantry, it is scholarlike in its criticisms."—*Record.*

WORKS PUBLISHED BY

TALES FROM ALSACE; or, Scenes and Portraits from
Life in the Days of the Reformation, as drawn from Old Chronicles. Translated from the German. Crown 8vo, 3s. 6d. cloth.
"We have not for a long time perused a more delightful book. . . . . we are certain wherever it is read it will be a great favourite with young and old."—*Daily Review.*

A MEMOIR OF THE LATE REV. DR. MALAN,
OF GENEVA. By one of his Sons. With Portrait and Engravings. Post 8vo, 7s. 6d. cloth.
"We feel ourselves in this biography brought into contact with an humble but truly saintly man, whom to know is to love, and whom it is impossible to know without being ourselves benefited."—*Christian Work.*

FAMILY PRAYERS FOR A MONTH, with a few
Prayers for Special occasions. By the Rev. J. W. REEVE, M.A., Portman Chapel. Small Crown 8vo, 3s. 6d. cloth.
"Admirably suited for the devotions of a Christian household."—*Rock.*

BEACONS OF THE BIBLE. By the Very Rev. HENRY
LAW, M.A., Dean of Gloucester, Author of "Christ is All," etc. Small Crown 8vo, 3s. 6d. cloth.
"Dr. Law's work overflows with striking and beautiful images, briefly expressed in short, incisive sentences, often musical in their cadence, and melodious as poetry itself."—*Rock.*

THE WORKS OF THE LATE JAMES HAMILTON,
D.D., F.L.S. Complete in Six Vols., post 8vo, each 7s. 6d. cloth.
"More than most men he has embalmed his qualities in his writings. . . They well deserve to be published in a permanent form, and this handsome library edition will be a great boon to many families."—*Freeman.*

OUR FATHER IN HEAVEN. The Lord's Prayer
Familiarly Explained and Illustrated. A Book for the Young. By the Rev. J. H. WILSON, Edinburgh. With Illustrations. Small Crown 8vo, 2s. 6d. cloth.
"We know no better book of its kind."—*Edinburgh Evening Courant.*
"One of the most interesting and successful expositions of the Lord's Prayer in our language."—*Evangelical Magazine.*

RIGHTS AND WRONGS; or, Begin at Home. By M. M.
GORDON, Author of "Work; Plenty to Do, and How to Do it." Small Crown 8vo, 2s. 6d. limp cloth.
"The purpose of the publication is for circulation amongst the female inmates of cottages and working men's houses, or to be read at mothers' or daughters' meetings. For these ends it will be found exceedingly suitable, and fitted to be widely useful."—*Aberdeen Free Press.*

FROM SEVENTEEN TO THIRTY. The Town Life
of a Youth from the Country; its Trials, Temptations, and Advantages. Lessons from the History of Joseph. By the Rev. THOMAS BINNEY. Small Crown 8vo, 1s. 6d. cloth.
"Nothing can exceed the quiet dignity, beauty, and simplicity of style in which this book is written. Not only is it a model of wise scriptural exposition, but we cannot at this moment recall anything that approaches it."—*English Independent.*

JAMES NISBET AND CO.

THE SABBATH-SCHOOL INDEX. Pointing out the History and Progress of Sunday Schools, with approved modes of Instruction, etc., etc. By R. G. PARDEE, A.M. With Introductory Preface by the Rev. J. H. WILSON, Edinburgh. Small Crown 8vo, 2s. 6d. cloth.

"The author has succeeded in an admirable manner in producing a work that will stand pre-eminently as the teacher's handbook. We have not found one subject of any importance to the teacher which he has not considered."—*Weekly Review.*

MEMORIES OF OLIVET. By the Rev. J. R. MACDUFF, D.D. With Vignette. Post 8vo, 6s. 6d. cloth.

"The almost photographic clearness with which every point around Jerusalem is described, and the frequent though unobtrusive illustration of the sacred text from eastern life, together with the vivid realization of the movements of our Saviour during the last few days of his earthly career, make the *Memories of Olivet* a most valuable companion in the study of the preacher and teacher, and in the chamber of the home student."—*Record.*

THE LIFE OF THE LATE REV. DR. MARSH, of Beddington. By his DAUGHTER, the Author of "English Hearts and English Hands," etc. With Portrait. Post 8vo, 10s. cloth; Cheap Edition, Small Crown 8vo, 3s. 6d. cloth.

"We have read this volume with much interest, and can recommend it as an excellent account of Dr. Marsh's life and career, and of the associations connected with them."—*Times.*

MEMORIES OF GENNESARET; or, Our Lord's Ministrations in Galilee. With a new and extended Preface, from observations made upon the spot. By the Rev. J. R. MACDUFF, D.D. Post 8vo, 6s. 6d. cloth.

"An excellent and exceedingly attractive work. Its character is simplicity, earnestness, and devotedness."—*Witness.*

THE PEARL OF PARABLES. Notes on the Parable of the Prodigal Son. By the late JAMES HAMILTON, D.D. With Twelve Illustrations by SELOUS. Printed on toned paper, and elegantly bound. Small 4to, 8s. 6d. cloth. Also a Cheap Edition, without Plates, 16mo, 1s. 6d. cloth.

"A book like this is a very rich enjoyment for both mind and heart. A more fitting gift-book for young men could hardly be conceived."—*British Quarterly Review.*

THE DARWINIAN THEORY OF THE TRANSMUTATION OF SPECIES EXAMINED. By a GRADUATE OF THE UNIVERSITY OF CAMBRIDGE. Demy 8vo, 10s. 6d. cloth.

"The volume is a work of no ordinary merit. . . . It indicates extensive reading, intimate acquaintance with the whole history of the Transmutation school of thinking, great mastery of the abundant material placed at the disposal of the author, and a large infusion of common sense."—*British Quarterly Review.*

PLAIN SERMONS ON THE GOSPEL MIRACLES. By the Rev. ARTHUR ROBERTS, M.A. Crown 8vo, 5s. cloth.

"Plain and simple, without attempt at critical disquisition or philosophical inquiry, they are earnest, scriptural, and attractive. The style, with nothing lofty in it, is pleasant, and the sermons are thoroughly readable."—*Church of England Magazine.*

WORKS PUBLISHED BY

THE SHADOW AND THE SUBSTANCE. A Second Series of Addresses by STEVENSON A. BLACKWOOD, Esq. Small Crown 8vo. 2s. cloth limp, 2s. 6d. cloth boards.

"A very thoughtful and thoroughly scriptural view of the Passover. . . . To those who wish for useful reading to adult classes, or to mothers' meetings, we commend this book."—*Record.*

THE PROPHET OF FIRE; or, The Life and Times of Elijah, and their Lessons. By the Rev. J. R. MACDUFF, D.D. Post 8vo, 6s. 6d. cloth.

"Full of incident, rich in illustration, smooth and pleasing in style, and abounding in practical lessons."—*English Presbyterian Messenger.*

THE PRAISE-BOOK; being "Hymns of Praise," with accompanying Tunes. By the Rev. W. REID, M.A. Harmonies written or revised by H. E. DIBDIN. Crown 4to, 7s. 6d. cloth elegant.

"This magnificent volume has no rival, at least we know of none published in England. It is a standard book both as to hymns and music."—*Sword and Trowel.*

ST. PAUL; His Life and Ministry to the Close of his Third Missionary Journey. By the Rev. THOMAS BINNEY. Crown 8vo, 5s. cloth.

"Mr. Binney has elaborated into a volume his magnificent lectures on St. Paul's Life and Ministry. . . Mr. Binney's books need no commendation of ours."—*Quarterly Messenger Young Men's Christian Association.*

SUNSETS ON THE HEBREW MOUNTAINS: or, Some of the most prominent Biographies of Sacred Story viewed from Life's Close. By the Rev. J. R. MACDUFF, D.D. Post 8vo, 6s. 6d. cloth.

"Dr. Macduff has rightly appreciated the characters he has described, and has truthfully delineated their features. The points of instruction, too, which he draws from them are apposite, scriptural, and telling."—*Church of England Magazine.*

THE LIGHTHOUSE; or, The Story of a Great Fight between Man and the Sea. By R. M. BALLANTYNE, Author of "The Lifeboat," etc., etc. Illustrations. Crown 8vo, 5s. cloth.

"Interesting to all readers."—*Arbroath Guide.*
"A story at once instructive and amusing."—*Dundee Advertiser.*

FIFTY-TWO SHORT SERMONS FOR FAMILY READING. By HORATIUS BONAR, D.D. Crown 8vo, 6s. cloth.

"These are short plain sermons for family reading, and are admirably fitted for so good a purpose."—*English Presbyterian Messenger.*

THE LIFEBOAT: A Tale of our Coast Heroes. A Book for Boys. By R. M. BALLANTYNE, Author of "The Lighthouse," etc. With Illustrations. Crown 8vo, 5s. cloth.

"This is another of Mr. Ballantyne's excellent stories for the young. They are all well written, full of romantic incidents, and are of no doubtful moral tendency; on the contrary, they are invariably found to embody sentiments of true piety, and manliness and virtue."—*Inverness Advertiser.*

FORGIVENESS, LIFE, AND GLORY. Addresses by S. A. BLACKWOOD, Esq. Small Crown 8vo, 2s. cloth limp; 2s. 6d. cloth boards.

"Full of devout earnestness and scriptural truth."—*Church of England Magazine.*
"They are all solemn and searching.—*Morning Advertiser.*

HYMNS OF FAITH AND HOPE. By Horatius Bonar,

D.D. First, Second, and Third Series, Crown 8vo, each 5s. cloth. Also, Pocket Editions, Royal 32mo, each 1s. 6d. Also a Royal Edition, printed at the Chiswick Press, and handsomely bound. Post 8vo, 7s. 6d. cloth.

"There is a freshness and vigour, an earnestness and a piety in these compositions, which is very gratifying. The language is highly poetical."—*Evangelical Christendom.*

THE POEMS OF GEORGE HERBERT. Illustrated

in the highest style of Wood Engraving, by Birket Foster, Clayton, and Noel Humphreys. Post 4to, 12s. cloth elegant.

"There have been many editions of Herbert's Poetical Works. One of the most splendid is that of Nisbet, London."—*Encyclopædia Britannica.*

ILLUSTRATIVE GATHERINGS FOR PREACH-

ERS AND TEACHERS. By the Rev. G. S. Bowes, B.A. First and Second Series, Small Crown 8vo, each, 3s. 6d. cloth.

"Its tone is thoroughly evangelical and spiritual, and it is fitted to furnish useful hints and illustrations to the Christian teacher."—*Christian Witness.*

ENGLISH HEARTS AND ENGLISH HANDS; or,

The Railway and the Trenches. By the Author of "Memorials of Captain Hedley Vicars." Small Crown 8vo, 5s. cloth. Also a Cheaper Edition, 2s. cloth limp.

"The Memorials of Vicars and these Memorials of the Crystal Palace Navvies are books of precisely the same type, and must not be overlooked. We recognize in them an honesty of purpose, a purity of heart, and a warmth of human affection, combined with a religious faith, that are very beautiful."—*Times.*

THE EXETER HALL LECTURES TO YOUNG

MEN, from their commencement in 1845-6, to their termination in 1864-5, all uniformly printed, and handsomely bound in cloth, and embellished with portraits of the Friends and Patrons of the Young Men's Christian Association. Complete in 20 vols., price of each volume, 4s.; or the whole series for £3.

MATTHEW HENRY'S COMMENTARY ON THE

HOLY BIBLE, comprising upwards of 7000 Pages, well printed (the Notes as well as the Text in clear and distinct type) on good paper, forming Nine Imperial 8vo volumes, and handsomely bound in cloth. Price £3 3s. cloth.

⁎ The work may also be had in a variety of extra bindings, of which a list will be forwarded on application.

THE REV. THOS. SCOTT'S COMMENTARY ON

THE HOLY BIBLE, comprising Marginal References, a copious Topical Index, Fifteen Maps, and Sixty-nine Engravings, illustrative of Scripture Incidents and Scenery. Complete in 6 vols. 4to, published at £4 4s., now offered for £2 10s.

THE BIBLE MANUAL: an Expository and Practical

Commentary on the Books of Scripture, arranged in Chronological Order: forming a Hand-book of Biblical Elucidation for the use of Families, Schools, and Students of the Word of God. Translated from the German Work, edited by the late Rev. Dr. C. G. Barth, of Calw, Wurtemberg. Imperial 8vo, 12s. cloth.

THE WORD SERIES.

By ELIZABETH WETHERALL and ANNA LOTHROP, Authors of "The Wide Wide World," "Dollars and Cents," etc. Uniform with the "Golden Ladder" Series, with Coloured Illustrations. Crown 8vo, each 3s. 6d. cloth.

"The aim of this series of volumes is so to set forth the Bible incidents and course of history, with its train of actors, as to see them in the circumstances and colouring, the light and shade of their actual existence."

1. WALKS FROM EDEN: The Scripture Story from the Creation to the Death of Abraham.
2. THE HOUSE OF ISRAEL: The Scripture Story from the Birth of Isaac to the Death of Jacob.
3. THE STAR OUT OF JACOB: The Scripture Story Illustrating the Earlier Portion of the Gospel Narrative.

THE GOLDEN LADDER SERIES.

Uniform in size and binding, with eight coloured Illustrations. Crown 8vo, cloth.

1. THE GOLDEN LADDER: Stories Illustrative of the Eight Beatitudes. By ELIZABETH and ANNA WARNER. 3s. 6d.
2. THE WIDE WIDE WORLD. By ELIZABETH WARNER. 3s. 6d.
3. QUEECHY. By the same. 3s. 6d.
4. MELBOURNE HOUSE. By the same. 3s. 6d.
5. DAISY. By the same. 3s. 6d.
6. THE OLD HELMET. By the same. 3s. 6d.
7. THE THREE LITTLE SPADES. By the same. 2s. 6d.
8. NETTIE'S MISSION: Stories Illustrative of the Lord's Prayer. By ALICE GRAY. 3s. 6d.
9. DAISY IN THE FIELD. By ELIZABETH WARNER. 3s. 6d.
10. STEPPING HEAVENWARD. By Mrs. PRENTISS. Author of "Little Susy." 2s. 6d.
11. WHAT SHE COULD, AND OPPORTUNITIES. Tales by ELIZABETH WARNER. 3s. 6d.
12. GLEN LUNA; or, Dollars and Cents. By ANNA WARNER. 3s. 6d.
13. DRAYTON HALL. Stories Illustrative of the Beatitudes. ALICE GRAY. 3s. 6d.
14. WITHOUT AND WITHIN. A New England Story. 3s. 6d.
15. VINEGAR HILL STORIES. Illustrative of the Parable of the Sower. By ANNA WARNER. 3s. 6d.
16. THE HOUSE IN TOWN. A Sequel to "Opportunities." By ELIZABETH WARNER. 2s. 6d.

JAMES NISBET AND CO.

THE ONE SHILLING JUVENILE SERIES.

Uniform in size and binding, 16mo, Illustrations, each 1s. cloth.

1. CHANGES UPON CHURCH BELLS. By C. S. H.
2. GONZALEZ AND HIS WAKING DREAMS. By C. S. H.
3. DAISY BRIGHT. By EMMA MARSHALL.
4. HELEN; or, Temper and its Consequences. By Mrs. G. GLADSTONE.
5. THE CAPTAIN'S STORY; or, The Disobedient Son. By W. S. MARTIN.
6. THE LITTLE PEATCUTTERS; or, The Song of Love. By EMMA MARSHALL.
7. LITTLE CROWNS, AND HOW TO WIN THEM. By the Rev. J. A. COLLIER.
8. CHINA AND ITS PEOPLE. By a MISSIONARY'S WIFE.
9. TEDDY'S DREAM; or, A Little Sweep's Mission.
10. ELDER PARK; or, Scenes in our Garden. By Mrs. ALFRED PAYNE, Author of "Nature's Wonders."
11. HOME LIFE AT GREYSTONE LODGE. By the Author of "Agnes Falconer."
12. THE PEMBERTON FAMILY, and other Stories.
13. CHRISTMAS AT SUNBURY DALE. By W. B. B., Author of "Clara Downing's Dream."
14. PRIMROSE; or, The Bells of Old Effingham. By Mrs. MARSHALL.
15. THE BOY GUARDIAN. By the Author of "Dick and his Donkey."
16. VIOLET'S IDOL. By JOANNA H. MATTHEWS.
17. FRANK GORDON. By the Author of "The Young Marooners." And LITTLE JACK'S FOUR LESSONS. By the Author of "The Golden Ladder."
18. THE COTTAGE ON THE CREEK. By the Hon. MRS. CLIFFORD-BUTLER.
19. THE WILD BELLS AND WHAT THEY RANG. By W. S. MARTIN.
20. TO-DAY AND YESTERDAY. A Story of Winter and Summer Holidays. By Mrs. MARSHALL.
21. GLASTONBURY; or the early British Christians.
22. MAX; a Story of the Oberstein Forest.

THE EIGHTEENPENNY JUVENILE SERIES.

Uniform in size and binding, 16mo, with Illustrations, each 1s. 6d. cloth.

1. AUNT EDITH; or, Love to God the Best Motive.
2. SUSY'S SACRIFICE. By Alice Gray.
3. KENNETH FORBES; or, Fourteen Ways of Studying the Bible.
4. LILIES OF THE VALLEY, and other Tales.
5. CLARA STANLEY; or, a Summer among the Hills.
6. THE CHILDREN OF BLACKBERRY HOLLOW.
7. HERBERT PERCY; or, From Christmas to Easter.
8. PASSING CLOUDS; or, Love conquering Evil.
9. DAYBREAK; or, Right Struggling and Triumphant.
10. WARFARE AND WORK; or, Life's Progress.
11. EVELYN GREY. By the Author of "Clara Stanley."
12. THE HISTORY OF THE GRAVELYN FAMILY.
13. DONALD FRASER. By the Author of "Bertie Lee."
14. THE SAFE COMPASS, AND HOW IT POINTS. By Rev. R. Newton, D.D.
15. THE KING'S HIGHWAY; or, Illustrations of the Commandments. By the same.
16. BESSIE AT THE SEASIDE. By Joanna H. Matthews.
17. CASPER. By the Authors of "The Wide Wide World," etc.
18. KARL KRINKEN; or, The Christmas Stocking. By the same.
19. MR. RUTHERFORD'S CHILDREN. By the same.
20. SYBIL AND CHRYSSA. By the same.

JAMES NISBET AND CO. 15

THE EIGHTEENPENNY JUVENILE SERIES—*Continued*.

21. HARD MAPLE. By the same.
22. OUR SCHOOL DAYS. Edited by C. S. H.
23. AUNT MILDRED'S LEGACY. By the Author of "The Best Cheer," etc.
24. MAGGIE AND BESSIE, AND THEIR WAY TO DO GOOD. By JOANNA H. MATTHEWS.
25. GRACE BUXTON; or, The Light of Home. By EMMA MARSHALL.
26. LITTLE KATY AND JOLLY JIM. By ALICE GRAY.
27. BESSIE AT SCHOOL. By JOANNA H. MATTHEWS.
28. BESSIE AND HER FRIENDS. By the same.
29. BESSIE IN THE MOUNTAINS. By the same.
30. HILDA AND HILDEBRAND; or, The Twins of Ferndale Abbey.
31. GLEN ISLA. By Mrs. DRUMMOND.
32. LUCY SEYMOUR; or, "It is more Blessed to give than to receive." By the same.
33. LOUISA MORETON; or, "Children, obey your Parents in all things." By the same.
34. THE WILMOT FAMILY; or, "They that deal truly are His delight." By the same.
35. SOWING IN TEARS, AND REAPING IN JOY. By FRANZ HOFFMANN. Translated from the German by Mrs. FABER.
36. BESSIE ON HER TRAVELS. By JOANNA H. MATTHEWS.
37. LITTLE NELLIE; or, The Clockmaker's Daughter.
38. THREE LITTLE SISTERS. By Mrs. MARSHALL, Author of "Daisy Bright."
39. MABEL GRANT. A Highland Story.
40. THE RETURN FROM INDIA. By the Author of "Hilda and Hildebrand," &c.
41. THE COURT AND THE KILN.
42. SILVER SANDS.
43. LIONEL ST CLAIR. By the Author of "Herbert Percy."

16 WORKS PUBLISHED BY JAMES NISBET AND CO.

THE SELECT SERIES.

Crown 8vo, each 3s. 6d. cloth. Bound by BURN. Most of them with Illustrations.

1. DERRY. A Tale of the Revolution. By CHARLOTTE ELIZABETH.
2. THE LAND OF THE FORUM AND THE VATICAN. By the Rev. NEWMAN HALL, LL.B.
3. THE LISTENER. By CAROLINE FRY.
4. DAYS AND NIGHTS IN THE EAST; or, Illustrations of Bible Scenes. By the Rev. HORATIUS BONAR, D.D.
5. BEECHENHURST. A Tale. By A. G., Author of "Among the Mountains," etc.
6. THE HOLY WAR. By JOHN BUNYAN.
7. THE PILGRIM'S PROGRESS. By JOHN BUNYAN.
8. THE MOUNTAINS OF THE BIBLE; Their Scenes and their Lessons. By the Rev. JOHN MACFARLANE, LL.D.
9. THROUGH DEEP WATERS; or, Seeking and Finding. An Autobiography.
10. HOME AND FOREIGN SERVICE; or, Pictures in Active Christian Life.
11. LIFE. A Series of Illustrations of the Divine Wisdom in the Forms, Structures, and Instincts of Animals. By PHILLIP H. GOSSE, F.R.S.
12. LAND AND SEA. By P. H. GOSSE, F.R.S.
13. JOHN KNOX AND HIS TIMES. By the Author of "The Story of Martin Luther," etc.
14. HOME IN THE HOLY LAND. By Mrs. FINN.
15. A THIRD YEAR IN JERUSALEM. A Tale Illustrating Incidents and Customs in Modern Jerusalem. By Mrs. FINN.
16 & 17. THE ROMANCE OF NATURAL HISTORY. By P. H. GOSSE, F.R.S. First and Second Series.
18. BYEWAYS IN PALESTINE. By JAMES FINN, Esq. F.R.A.S., late H M. Consul of Jerusalem and Palestine.
19. HEADS AND TALES; or, Anecdotes and Stories of Quadrupeds and other Beasts, as connected with the Histories of more or less distinguished men. Selected and written by ADAM WHITE, Duddingston.
20. BLOOMFIELD. A Tale by ELIZABETH WARREN, Author of "John Knox and his Times," &c.
21. TALES FROM ALSACE; or, Scenes and Portraits from Life in the Days of the Reformation, as drawn from old Chronicles. Translated from the German.
22. HYMNS OF THE CHURCH MILITANT. By the Author of "The Wide Wide World."
23. THE PHYSICIAN'S DAUGHTERS; or, The Spring Time of Woman. By the Author of "Wandering Homes and their Influences," &c.

Henderson, Rait, & Fenton, Printers, 23, Berners Street, Oxford Street.

www.ingramcontent.com/pod-product-compliance
Lightning Source LLC
Chambersburg PA
CBHW031904220426
43663CB00006B/763